THE BEST ADVICE I EVER GOT

THE BEST ADVICE I EVER GOT

TERRY PRONE

CURRACH
PRESS

First published in 2007 by
CURRACH PRESS
55A Spruce Avenue, Stillorgan Industrial Park, Blackrock, Co. Dublin
www.currach.ie

1 3 5 4 2

Cover by Sin é Design
Origination by Currach Press
Printed by Betaprint, Bluebell Industrial Estate, Dublin 12
ISBN: 978 1 85607 954 9
The author has asserted her moral rights.

FOR THE SKIN AND BLISTER, HILARY KENNY

ACKNOWLEDGEMENTS

The quoted advice in this book is gratefully acknowledged, as is the willngness to be harassed of many individuals whose favourite piece of advice was – for various reasons – unprintable.

Portions of this book appeared in different forms in *The Irish Examiner* and *Image* magazine.

Contents

INTRODUCTION

Most people who have been offering a service for a long time get more confident the longer they do it. Exceptions happen, though.

I've been in the advice business since I was a teenager, and the longer I do it, the more scared I get. Because when you give advice, you're interfering in someone else's life. Interfering with the best of intentions, but what's the road to hell paved with? Good intentions.

Most advice gets ignored or forgotten, but now and then someone will tell me (or more often, tell my husband, Tom Savage) that they were on a course twenty years ago, and something said to them changed their life. Sometimes, they tell me I spotted some talent in them that nobody other than their mother/wife/best friend ever believed they had, and as a result, they got enough confidence to get a degree, seek promotion, or set up their own business. I'm thrilled – and my legs begin to shake, as I think, 'Oh, Jasus, how did I know that back then? How could I have been so sure? Say if they'd been fired? Or set up their business and gone bankrupt?'

The real killer is when they quote a bit of advice given by me to their mother or father. I figure it will be time to retire when someone tells me I came up with a wonderful bit of advice that changed the life of their grandfather or grandmother.

Advice is like garlic. A little of it is good for you. Just enough of it tastes wonderful. Too much of it makes you feel ropy and makes other people want to edge away from you.

This book is a sampler of advice on various aspects of the way we live, with examples from people in different walks of life of the advice they believe was the best they ever got.

I hope you find something life-changing in it. And, on the way, encounter something that makes you think or laugh or both.

1

Timing Is Everything

Advice is like joke-telling: timing is everything. Advice offered before it is wanted is like one of those jokes about the groom, told by the best man, which not only gives the groom's mother a lot more information about her adored offspring than she ever needed, but gives the bride and the bride's parents a surfeit of nasty.

The problem with advice-giving is that it's so pleasurable. When it comes to advice, it really is more blessed to give than to receive. Having information which could conceivably be useful to someone else and not giving it to them is like carrying a loaded rucksack around. The giver assumes the recipient will be grateful. It isn't always the case.

Witness the Sherlock Holmes story where Watson realises that Holmes cannot name the planets of the solar system. Worse, the pipe-puffing detective genius doesn't even know that the earth orbits around the sun. Watson, understandably, wants to get busy fixing this information gap, and is amazed to meet with resistance. Holmes has to explain to him that his mind is like an attic with a limited amount of storage space, where he keeps the stuff that will help him when he sets out to catch the bad guys. Knowing the names of the planets or the fact that the sun stays still while the earth runs rings around it is of no functional value to him. Now that

Watson has loaded this unnecessary information into his mental attic, Holmes is going to have to work hard at unloading it and forgetting it.

Much good advice doesn't get used because the person on the receiving end doesn't have the wherewithal to use it. It's a bit like giving one of those easy-to-use battery-powered can openers to someone with arthritis. As far as the giver is concerned, it's a stroke of genius. It's going to make the arthritic person's life so much easier. They can't figure why, three weeks later, it's still sitting, unopened, on a shelf. The reason, of course, is that the bloody thing comes in a hard moulded plastic blister pack the arthritic person can't undo.

At a corporate level, the equivalent, generously given and just as useless, is the change management course. Over the past ten to fifteen years, change management courses have been provided in almost every area of industry in this country with the best intentions and virtually no end results. That's because change management courses basically tell workers to be more flexible. An excellent piece of advice, based on historic evidence. The Romans, for example, while highly disciplined and systematic, were outstandingly flexible, adapting to different forms of warfare, including naval battles, as they encountered different enemies. Alexander the Great beat the Persian army, even though it was much bigger than his own, because he had trained his soldiers to be mobile and opportunistic. Since the industrial revolution, the businesses that have survived have been able to react fluidly to a changed external context.

The difficulty with change management training is that delivering it to a workforce accustomed, all its working life, to obeying orders and fulfilling routine tasks gives them new words for what they still can't do. They end up able to quote case studies. They can warble about who moved their cheese. But they never turn into flexible, adaptive, positive embracers of change.

One of the best bits of advice about giving advice is: until the person knows they have a problem, don't offer a solution. And, if you get started because someone asked you for advice, as a man named Haskins once observed, 'the time to stop talking is when the other person nods his head affirmatively but says nothing.'

People frequently already own the information wannabe advisers long to tell them. For example, Valerie Bertinelli, the American TV actress who starred in *One Day at a Time*, recently became a spokesperson for a slimming organisation, having lost thirty of the pounds she had gained since her days of stardom. She comments bitterly about the 'advice' and 'help' offered to her, during her fat years, by perfect strangers who recognised her.

'What always got me,' she says, 'was someone would come up to me and say, "I think you've put on a few pounds." Really? Because I don't own a mirror? I know – believe me!'

While unasked-for criticism dressed up as advice coming from strangers is motivated by anything from simple bitchiness to earnest meddling, an awful lot of advice coming from businesses is motivated by corporate self-protection. The phrases of this kind of advice are familiar to all of us: Terms and Conditions Apply. Always Read the Instructions. From this category comes arguably the daftest and least productive piece of advice ever given: Do Not Try This at Home.

On the other hand, the non-judgemental movement has now reached such a point that, if you consult with a counseller to help you get your head straight around a problem, the chances are that, even if you pay them, they won't give you advice, bopping your question back to you with another: 'What do you think, yourself?'

A good rule of thumb about giving advice is to make sure, first of all, that you're being asked for advice. Many people – particularly women – want to talk out a problem, rather than be handed the answer to it, QED. Indeed, that's one of the recurring complaints by women about men: that they too briskly get to the recommendation for corrective action, when what the woman wanted was a listening ear and no more than that. If someone doesn't specifically ask for advice, don't give it.

Even if someone does ask for advice, go around the houses a bit before you lash it at them. 'I want to ask your advice' is a popular conversational opener which means the sum total of feck all. Ask at least five questions before you allow yourself even to think about making proposals for solving the problem. That way, if you eventually become an adviser, you will have a more acute sense of the nature of the problem and the characteristics of the person who has it, enabling you to hit the spot in a way that just might lead to changed behaviour. And, while you're at it, ask yourself a question: Is there anything I could do that would be more helpful, in real terms, than giving advice? If the answer is yes, do it.

Psychotherapists have found huge cultural variations in the way individuals experience their bad times. Studies into post traumatic stress disorder, for example, found that, while people in Sri Lanka were grievously affected after the tsunami there, their symptoms and concerns didn't match those reported by, among others, soldiers traumatised by the Vietnam war. Salvadorean women refugees reported feelings of great heat as a sequel to their suffering, while Cambodians, after Pol Pot, reported nocturnal visits by evil spirits. The bottom line is that the kind of counselling, therapy or advice offered to someone in one country or belonging to one race will not necessarily serve someone whose mindset is quite different.

Older people, for example, find intolerable the advice they get from younger people on how to cope with diminished short-term memory. That advice usually starts with the younger person announcing that they, too, forget things, and goes on to propose that the older person make lists of items they might forget and use Post-IT notes stuck at relevant points in the house to serve as memory triggers. One woman in her late eighties, promising to choke the next proponent of Post-IT notes she meets, says that younger advice-givers haven't the beginnings of an understanding of the cluster of hindrances posed by memory loss due to age.

'Of course I use yellow sticky notes,' she says. 'And then, days later, I come across a note that says 'Don't forget thermostat.' It's heavily underlined, so I know it's important. I just don't know what it means. I obviously knew what it meant when I wrote it, but when I find it, for the life of me, I can't work out which thermostat I should be mindful of. My whole house is dotted with yellow stickies with names on them, lists on them, and perhaps one in ten serves the purpose it's supposed to. All the others just make me anxious.'

The writer Floyd Skloot would agree with her. Brain-damaged as a result of an accident, he is constantly at the receiving end of maddening advice from people who tell him the daily problems thrown up by his intellectual deficit are no problem, that the kind of embarrassing amnesic episodes that dot his life happen to them, too. He sadly acknowledges:

> I know, it happens to everyone. But not as the norm, not predictably. If it were only a problem with short-term memory, I don't think I would mind it so much when people say, 'Oh, I do that all the time.' I would be able to stop myself from telling them, 'Well, I didn't! Not until December 7, 1988.' If it were only short-term memory that was my problem, I might not say, 'Yeah, well, can you learn how to use a new camera or boom box? Can you compute change from a ten-dollar purchase? Do you lose the fifty dollars you had in your pocket while

you're browsing through a bookstore? Do you forget
phone numbers in the act of dialing them? Do you get
lost in your own neighborhood? Do you call your cat by
the name of the dog you had ten years ago?'

Moral? Don't try to generate commonality with someone by
claiming to suffer from whatever ails them. It will make any advice
you offer unacceptable, as well as infuriating them.

It's also important for advice-givers not to kid themselves that
because they have the data, they will change someone else's life.
Think of the smoker. Most of the addicted smokers around us are
all too aware of the data. They know precisely what smoking does
to them in the present time, just as they are aware of the trouble
they are storing up for themselves in the future by their habit. But
that information, *on its own*, does not magically convert smokers
into non-smokers. Beware of believing that because something is
obvious, inescapable and imperative to you, it is necessarily obvious,
inescapable and imperative to everybody else. It isn't, and presenting
it as if it was can lose you friends.

Great advisers develop the capacity to stand in the other
person's shoes. Lousy advisers give themselves away as lacking that
capacity, when they say things like, 'Well, I'd just say to him…' or, 'If
I were you, what I would do is…' You're *not* them. Even if you came
from the same family, you weren't raised the same way: younger
siblings have a different experience of parenthood and family life
from their older brothers and sisters. The pressures, constraints and
consequences for you are not the same as they are for the person
you are advising. So work out in your head the likely outcomes for
them before you start ladling out prescriptions.

And, while we're on the subject of prescriptions, be conscious
that when people are upset or fearful about an issue in their lives,

this emotional turmoil inhibits their listening and recollection processes. This truth emerged from medicine, where it was found that one of the reasons patients with dangerously high blood pressure were often 'non-compliant' – in other words, did not take their pills in the way and at the time they were supposed to take them, or didn't take them at all – was that the day the regimen was introduced to them, typically, was the day the diagnosis was shared with them.

Being told you have dangerously high blood pressure panics many patients, who immediately think of the stroke which paralysed their grandmother or robbed their grandfather of speech. In that initial panic, they are unlikely to pay much attention to the details of medicine-ingestion. So if you give advice to someone who's in a blue funk, don't be surprised if they don't follow through, and don't be irritated if they later tell you they did follow through, when you know damn well they didn't. They may not have registered what you actually said to them at the time.

Advice is a gift that must be asked for. It should be asked for several times. It should be delivered without strings attached. You're not a judge, advising someone to quit alcohol and attaching a monitor to their ankle to make sure they do it. Offer what you can. Don't compare yourself with the person to whom you are giving the advice. Don't ask them afterwards what they did about it. Like all gifts, advice should be lightly given and the adviser should not take it personally if the recipient swaps it for something that fits them better.

P.G. Wodehouse, author
I always advise people not to give advice.

Ambrose Bierce, author
Consult, a definition: To seek another's approval of a course already decided on.

Benjamin Franklin, statesman and author
Wise men don't need advice. Fools don't take it.

Bill Cosby, comedian
A word to the wise isn't necessary, it's the stupid ones who need all the advice.

Erica Jong, author
Advice is what we ask for when we already know the answer but wish we didn't.

François de la Rochefoucauld, author
Old people give advice to console themselves for no longer being able to set a bad example.

2

The Best Advice I (Personally) Ever Got

My mother had a way of giving advice that made her sound like a cross between Lady Bracknell and the Delphic Oracle. There was no arguing with her advice. It wasn't the word of God. It was the word of God's superior.

She specialised in reactive advice. Present her with a situation and she knew the rules applying to that situation. Present her with a problem, and she not only knew how to solve it, she knew what regulations you'd broken to cause the problem. Present her with a gift and you might get, in return, a Great Truth. I came home from school one day, suffused with pride, clutching a doiley I had crocheted for her. She turned it over and admired the stitching in a measured way. Years later, when reading Dr Johnson's observation about women preaching, an almost audible click went off in my head. Johnson likened it to dogs walking on their hind legs, saying that it was never done well, but you were surprised to find it done at all. That was precisely the attitude my mother had brought to praising my little doiley.

Nettled, at the time, by her palpable lack of enthusiasm, I demanded to know what was wrong with the crochet. Nothing, she admitted. She would put it on her dressing table.

'But?' I prodded. (I spent my childhood on the edge of a precipice of disapproval dug by my mother, masochistically requesting permission to fall right down into it.)

'Never do anything a machine can do better and cheaper,' she said crisply.

Now, lest you think my mother's advice was crushing to her children, it was, in fact, rather more nuanced in its impact. Before I'd got into the crocheting, I had learned to knit. Crack cocaine had nothing on the addictive powers of knitting, for me. I'd have got up in the middle of the night to knit, and did.

Following a pattern, on the other hand, was like reading the instructions to a new gadget. OK, you'd end up with a properly-assembled functional end result, but the tedium...So instead of a pair of baby bootees or a scarf, I knit a girl. Not just any girl. A dancing girl. A ballerina in a tutu *en pointe*. If you wanted to, you could make the girl's hands go over her head and join there – I left a little wool to allow for them to be tied together.

My mother discovered this artefact a few days later. I found her standing stock-still in the kitchen, looking at it as if it held the third (or is it the fourth?) secret of Fatima. She looked from the knitted girl to me and I tried to figure out what rule I'd broken in the girl's production. Maybe you weren't supposed to do representational art in wool. Maybe it was like those primitive peoples who don't like to have their photograph taken lest it steals away their soul.

'You are creative,' she told me, in a tone somewhere between an ultimatum and a death sentence. 'Do not ever waste your time on anything uncreative.'

She took the little blue dancer, hand-washed her with infinite care, dried her out and flattened her like a flower between the pages of a book.

My mother was so sure of every stricture she laid on my sister and me that we both assumed she had a direct line at least to the

Almighty, and probably (given her capacity to catch us doing bad things) to the FBI as well. Her instructions marched singly, building up gradually into an army of axioms designed to keep us safe from disease, disaster, academic failure, vulgarity and ourselves.

'If you start to read a book, you must finish it,' was one of those instructions. To this day, no matter how bad a book is, I finish it for fear I'll be struck by a thunderbolt for ditching it. She did make an exception of a writer named Erle Stanley Gardner. If you were dumb enough to start one of his tripe-offerings, you were allowed to pitch it from you when you wised up enough to know it was garbage.

'The only fabrics to be worn next to the skin are the natural ones,' she advised.

This had its benefits and downsides. It kept Hilary and me clear of nylon knickers and bras, but subjected us to many pre-teen years of woollen vests which itched to the point of insanity.

My mother was never discountenanced, even when we were. My sister, having put in roughly fifteen perfect years from birth onwards as the kind of sweet-natured, polite, obliging, clever and diligent child hated by her peers because their mothers kept demanding why they couldn't be like 'that nice Hilary Prone?' mislaid her marbles briefly in secondary school. She let on to have lost something that she hadn't actually lost, and the nun at the receiving end of the 'explanation,' a woman of height and hauteur named Sr Annunciata, called her on it. If it was lost, as Hilary maintained, in the school, all she had to do was a bit of search and it would turn up, wouldn't it? Hilary nodded silently and embarked on what turned into weeks of predictably fruitless searching.

At some point in the saga, my mother found out what was going on, and Hilary got some crystal-clear advice from her on telling the truth and knowing when to cut your losses. The thrilling bit, however, was my mother sallying forth to the Holy Faith Convent and demanding Annunciata's presence. Annunciata's hauteur went soggy in the face of my mother's advice, delivered with quiet certainty, that failure to deliver the teaching she was paid to deliver on the pretext of teaching a silly adolescent a lesson would not go down well with the Department of Education, were they to hear about it, and she would do well to stop it immediately. Hilary was back in class within the hour, having ground her way through the requisite apology.

It was my mother's certitude that always made her advice so impelling. She was never visited by doubt. She always seemed to know the law (civil and Canon), the etiquette (Nancy Mitford the most-quoted source) and the financial implications (pocket-money fine) attached to any misdemeanour, and would apply whichever matched the crime, once she had the facts. She took a standard police approach, issuing a formal warning before she interrogated you and brushing aside anything other than hard data. Once she had the data, there was no stopping her. She went immediately into either punishment or protection mode.

One of the actions she took in protection mode was another sally forth to a school, this time on my behalf, just after my Confirmation. I'd been put on the outside of a seat in the church. That was where they put pupils who were good at learning stuff off by heart and who could therefore be relied on to produce the right answer out of the catechism when asked by the bishop in the aisle.

Except that, on the day, it wasn't a bishop. We got short-changed on the robes and solemnity, getting a substitute curate who was informal and easy-going. He stopped in front of me and asked my name.

'Well, Terry,' he said. 'Would you like a question on supernatural grace?'

'Not particularly, Father,' I answered. Truthfully.

He roared laughing.

'In that case, I'd better pick something else,' he said and asked me a quite different question which I answered perfectly.

I thought the next day in school would be great, as a result. Instead, I got sent home with a note to my mother. I handed it over. She unsealed it and read it in total silence.

'Put your coat back on,' she ordered. 'We're going down to that school this minute.'

When we arrived, the teacher in charge of our class told the rest of them to read the next page of the books in front of them and came out into the corridor, glowing in anticipation of grovelling apologies from my mother. My mother produced the note.

'It says here that when the priest asked her if she would like a question on supernatural grace, Terry said, "I'm not particular."'

'That's right.'

'No, it is not right,' my mother said icily. 'My daughter would never use that phraseology. Ever. "I'm not particular." Terry would never say anything so ungrammatical. I have no doubt that what she said was, "Not particularly, Father."'

The teacher looked confused. The last thing she'd expected was an exposition on grammar, and, the way she saw it, the issue was impertinence, not phraseology.

'Let us be clear,' my mother went on. 'If a priest asks a pupil, at an examination designed to ascertain that this pupil has reached the age of reason, a question seeking to elicit a preference, it is absolutely correct for that pupil to express such a preference. We will hear no more of this nonsense.'

I would say that 'she turned on her heel' and swept out of the school, except that I've never seen anybody successfully turn on a heel. She certainly swept out of the school, though. Nobody could sweep like my mother. I was constantly galloping after her when she did a magisterial sweep, because she had a good turn of speed as well as a touch of grandeur.

Throughout the weeks of frozen exclusion that teacher subsequently inflicted on me, I would cup my hand over my mouth so my left ear would fill with my whisper, and repeat Mamma's phrases: an examination designed to ascertain and seeking to elicit a preference.

The only time she blew it, in the advice-giving arena, was when I was too young to ask the question I asked at the tea table. I was four.

'Where do babies come from?'

My father suddenly needed to re-fill the marmalade dish. My sister got an odd attack of something between snorts and sneezes. My mother glared at them, drew a deep breath and – untypically – started in the wrong place.

'Well, you know where kittens come from?'

I nodded enthusiastically.

'It's the same with babies,' she began.

'From cats?' I shrilled.

At that point, my sister's snort/sneeze attack threatened to kill her before my mother could, and my father created a diversion by dropping the pot of marmalade all over the lino floor.

On all other occasions, my mother's advice was spot-on. Ladybirds were good; wasps were bad. Television rotted the mind. If you wanted good oratory, listen to James Dillon. Plastic shoes made your feet sweat. (Sorry. Perspire.) 'Pleased to meet you,' was not the proper way to greet someone. Breathing in and out of a paper bag cured hiccups. As long as you believed in Santa Claus, he existed. You could tell the priest anything in confession and he wouldn't be shocked because he'd heard much worse. Ornaments of any kind were clutter. Bamboo furniture held dust. Wearing anything with a brand name turned you into an unpaid promoter of the brand and no daughter of hers…

The fact that it was spot-on didn't mean that either of her daughters followed all her advice. Like all offspring, we did a pick-and-mix. One of the pieces of advice in which she particularly believed was that, when you were cooking, you should 'clean as you go.'

I didn't clean as I went. If I fry you an egg, at the end of the enterprise, the kitchen is going to look like a deranged bison has been doing salsa dancing on every surface.

On the other hand, if you happen to arrive in my home post-egg-cooking, I will not apologise to you for the state of the place, because my mother hammered into me that you should never apologise for your home. I've no idea why not, but it's very handy if your home most of the time looks like the local landfill, as mine does: my father's only advice to my husband-to-be, when they discussed the wisdom of marrying me, was to tell Tom that if he wanted to live in a pigsty, that was OK with my father.

Parental advice may become part of the warp and weave of our minds while not translating into behaviours. A bit like W.H. Auden's description of a professor as 'one who talks in someone else's sleep'. Throughout our lives, in a phantom replay, we hear our mother's voices telling us what to do in a given situation, while we go ahead and do precisely the opposite. My husband maintains that the best advice he ever got was from his mother.

'To hell with casting up,' was Mag Savage's great phrase.

'Casting up' was what marriage counsellors and psychotherapists today would call 'kitchen sinking'. That's where, in the middle of a fight about a specific issue, one person brings up everything the other person has ever done wrong, going back (in the case of a married couple) to when they were courting.

It's a problem for two reasons. First of all, it adds fuel to a blaze that might naturally die down, complicating a real and present issue with bitterly recollected past crimes. More importantly, it indicates a lack of forgiveness, one of the most useful virtues. Or, worse still, indicates that forgiveness, once granted, doesn't include forgetfulness, and so the original offence can be recycled indefinitely.

Mag Savage's advice may be five words long, but has dozens of trailing implications. Forgive and forget. Deal with the problem in front of you. Don't make things worse than they are. Don't store bitter memories for later use; it diminishes you and ends up demonstrating something much worse about you than it does about the person who perpetrated the original misdeed.

Sometimes, of course, advice doesn't come in words, but in actions. My father, despite his unheeded but grimly remembered warning to Tom, was not much of a man for giving advice. Orders, yes; advice, no. But the way he acted was advice in itself. Instead of that idiot suggestion, 'Just be yourself,' the advice his life gave me was, 'Never be like anybody else.' Which, if you think about it, makes a lot more sense to a kid growing up than being told to be themselves, when they don't know the hell who they are and when, as adolescents, they have at least six different selves to choose from, including their classroom self, the self they play when with friends, the self they try out with peers of the opposite sex, the self they present to parents and the self they wonder about in moments of rejection, despair and doubt.

My father's position in life was devil's advocate. The devil's advocate was a role given to a clergyman to act during the process leading up to a canonisation. When everybody else was presenting evidence that Joe Bloggs should become Saint Joe because of his impermeable faith or his unequalled corporal works of mercy (whatever the hell they were), the devil's advocate would rubbish Joe, seeking out any bit of evidence which would tarnish the Blogg reputation and insidiously suggesting sordid and squalid motivations for some of Joe's apparently benign actions.

Dad did devil's advocate on a daily basis. He did it opportunistically: whenever the be-suited lads from the Church of Latter-Day Saints would arrive at our door in lockstep, he would welcome them with so much enthusiasm, the Mormons must have thought they had a convert here just waiting to happen. He would then spend an hour or more poking holes in their arguments until they eventually got the message that he was trying to unconvert them.

He also did it reactively. In 1957, when the Russians announced that they had sent a satellite into space, the four of us heard the news from Radio Éireann's eight o'clock bulletin. My sister, something of an innovation and aviation nerd, was chuffed.

My father scoffed. A satellite? How gullible could she be? Put up by the Russians? (This from a man who for years promoted the notion that communism under Stalin was probably fine and dandy, if you could get past the misinformation put out by capitalist countries like Ireland.)

'You heard the announcer,' my sister said, getting redder in the face and shorter in the breath with rage. 'If we go out tonight at a quarter to ten, we'll be able to see it passing overhead.'

'There will be clouds tonight,' my father predicted. 'You'll see nothing and then they'll say it was just because of the clouds. But they picked a night that there would be clouds. There's no satellite. Where's the proof?'

'That's like saying Australia doesn't exist,' Hilary said, gathering up her schoolbag and heading for the bus. My father, shrugging into his overcoat and pulling his leather gloves out of the pocket, followed her, saying that he had serious doubts about Australia, too.

The best advice I ever got I got about ten years later, when I was sixteen. In 1966, Radio Éireann decided to stop being sporadic about its daily broadcasting. Up to that point, they came on the air in the morning to the repeated notes of 'O'Donnell Abú'. Half the people of Ireland developed what the Germans call an 'earworm' as a result: a little musical phrase that repeats in your head for half the day.

Having given the news and the weather forecast, the national broadcasting station then went off the air for the rest of the morning, and in our house, it was over to the BBC Home Service, where we heard short stories, documentaries, *Workers' Playtime*, and a soap opera called *Mrs Dale's Diary*, the signature tune of which was a signal to my mother to sit down and have her first cigarette of the day.

Radio Éireann came back on the air at lunchtime with news, a radio essay called *Topical Talk* and sponsored programmes, each of which was fifteen minutes long. A sponsored programme could be an agony aunt or general music. Then they shut down again until teatime.

In 1966, they decided to do what they announced as 'Round the Clock Radio.' It was round the clock for only about twelve hours, but it still meant new programmes at times where no programme had ever gone before. About a month before this became known, the phone rang in our house one evening, and when I picked it up, the caller, who had a whispery Cork voice, announced himself as Donncha O'Dulaing.

'Oh, go to hell, Niall, you can't catch me on that one,' I responded. Niall Buggy, one of the most gifted mimics who ever lived, was one of my colleagues in the Abbey Theatre School of Acting at the time. He was notorious for ringing friends up and letting on to be someone else. Usually someone more important than himself.

The Cork-voiced caller sounded a bit taken aback, but persisted. He was Donncha O'Dulaing from Radio Éireann, he said, where he was Head of Features.

'Niall, this isn't one of your better imitations,' I told him. 'I could do a better Donncha O'Dulaing myself.'

At this point, the caller asked me to write down a number and ring it and ask for Donncha O'Dulaing and told me he looked forward to hearing from me. (The same thing happened, much later, in the movie *The American President*, to Annette Bening when Michael Douglas was looking for a date with her.) I sat at the little telephone table in the hall, looking at the number I had written down, awash in doubt, terror and a blush that started in my socks. I rang the number.

'Radio Éireann,' a bright female voice stated.

I asked to speak with Donncha O'Dulaing and got put through. He laughed off my apologies and came to the point. Radio was very soon going to be on in the afternoon, and one of the new weekly programmes, called *The Young Idea*, needed a presenter. Would I be interested?

Would I what?

Well, would I meet him and my producer in the restaurant above the Capitol Cinema at lunchtime the following day?

Of course. No problem. Be delighted. I then went off in a complete state of confusion, trying to pick something to wear appropriate for a Lunch with a Departmental Head and a Producer, having never had a Lunch with anybody before. My search wasn't helped by my not obeying my mother's clean as you go advice, because picking something to wear meant searching through the six layers of debris on my bedroom floor to find a garment that wasn't covered in melted chocolate. (I was a messy sneak-eater.) Nor was it helped by my fury at Niall Buggy. OK, he hadn't made this particular phone call, but if he wasn't in the habit of practical jokes, I wouldn't be in this jam, would I?

I shouldn't remember the food, but – story of my life – I always remember the food. Chicken Maryland. It had fried banana on it. I couldn't get over it. Fruit, in the middle of a main course, and fried, at that. This had to be the acme of sophistication and it tasted wonderful, too.

Donncha O'Dulaing was fine but my producer terrified me. He had this shock of ash-blond hair and a chin on him like a shovel and when he spoke, it was in a growl. Not that he spoke much. Most of the time, he just looked at me from under his eyebrows as if I was a scientific specimen. Of some life-threatening bacterium.

Once I started to work with him, I found out that he was brand-new to this radio lark, too, and just as amazed as I was that he'd landed the gig. I'd been on a couple of TV programmes. So had he – singing with a guitar. But whereas my limited fame was positive, his was not. He had been a leader of USI, the student's union, and had a track record of radicalism. Radio Éireann were taking something of a risk in employing a left-leaning figure like Howard Kinlay, and Howard was terrified, that first day, that he'd say something that would lose him the job before he ever got a programme on the air. He was also terrified of me, because I had switched into bubbly/amusing mode and he thought I was like that all the time and how would he work with me without braining me for this babble?

The two of us started to get programmes on the air, unconstrained by any clue as to what we were about. A producer who was also a greyhound racing commentator named Pádraig O'Neill (Paddy O'Brien when he was being a commentator) did wander by a studio one day when we were editing a tape and murmur gently that I should never feel I was broadcasting to the whole of Ireland: 'Just one listener at a time.' Apart from that good advice, we were on our own. We made all the mistakes possible, which allowed the sound technicians to rescue us, which is what sound technicians like doing almost as much as they like *not* rescuing broadcasters who know it all.

One of the mistakes was getting close to the sea elephant seal in the Zoo. I was interviewing this animal's keeper, who adored the great slab of blubber. When I was finished, Howard started to disconnect the Uher tape recorder.

'Hey, why don't I interview the seal?' I asked. 'Ask him questions and get the noises he makes?'

In no time at all I was inside the enclosure holding a microphone in front of the seal, who was vast and possessed of fangs the size of lampposts. The keeper was a bit bothered about breaking the rules, but completely confident that the seal posed no danger to me. At one point, the seal opened a mouth that was mesmerising in scale and filth and emitted an opinion on a exhalation reeking of putrefaction.

'Jesus,' I said into the microphone. 'Jesus, the smell of him.'

It took Howard nearly an hour to remove the Holy Name from the tape. If it had gone out on the air, we were fired. I hovered, apologising. When the task was complete, he sat back and beamed at me. 'I really like workin' with you, you know that?'

I burbled in embarrassment. I was a fat sixteen-year old without much experience of compliments. True, one of my mother's bits of advice had always been that when someone compliments you, you must never contradict them but accept the compliment graciously. I knew the rule, all right, I just couldn't get the behaviour in place. Howard watched my floundering with some amusement, then got serious.

'Whenever you like someone, or whenever you find you love someone,' he growled, 'tell them. Tell them right then and there. Don't put it off. Don't tell other people but not tell them. You know why? Because life is awful short and someone could die without knowing you admired them. Or liked them. Or loved them.'

I thought out of that control room would I never get, what with compliments and advice on how to prevent people dying unfulfilled by the knowledge that I was fond of them. But it stuck. I started to do it, discovering, in the process, that it often comes as an astonishing and welcome surprise to the recipient. We're great at telling people what they're doing wrong. We're fantastic, especially if you pour a couple of pints and a modicum of grievance into us, at telling people they're the scum of the earth and shouldn't be allowed to live. But telling people we like them, admire them or love them is a risky proposition that can make us look seriously uncool, so we don't do it. And anyway, the person knows without us telling them, don't they? Of course they do. Or should, if they were paying attention.

Over time, the advice, acted on every day, every week, became a reflex. With wonderful consequences. Unguardedly telling a man I loved him put me in a situation where he told me he loved me back. Howard Kinlay's advice led to Tom Savage marrying me, which was a very good thing from my point of view. It had its downsides, of course. Like the week when Tom went into hospital for tests. The same week Howard went into a different hospital, also for tests. Tom had stomach cancer and eventually got out of the hospital. Howard, in his early forties, had lung cancer and didn't. (Tom had smoked forty cigarettes a day from his teen years. Howard never smoked tobacco but was a weekend marijuana-smoker.)

Before Howard knew the results of his tests, I visited him and he walked me to the door of St Vincent's afterwards, asking about

Tom. I told him how important his advice had been in my life. He didn't remember giving it.

'Jaysus,' he said. 'Did one thing right, anyway.'

And walked slowly back up to the ward, shaking his head over having given a bit of advice that had changed someone else's life for the better.

Adrienne Murphy, journalist

'You have a gift for words and stories. You should read a lot, and you should write.' That was the best career advice I ever got. It came from a hip young Joni Mitchell-type woman with long blonde hair, fabulously flaired jeans and platform boots. She drove a two-seater 1970 Datsun sportscar – the same as my dad – and she taught me how to read in a Boston state school when I was five years old. A year later my family moved back to Ireland. I never saw my teacher again. She was a beautiful angel who inspired me at a very early age to be a writer.

In career terms, Jim, the lovely boyfriend that I had when I was twenty years old, is a close second place to my angel-teacher. He urged me to interview Trenchtown, a ska band from Drogheda, for a student magazine that his pal edited. In the end my article wasn't used, and he submitted it to *Hot Press* magazine instead. *Hot Press* published it and my freelance writing career began.

Hitting my thirties, my career path became eclipsed by a spiritual journey. A seven-year patch of good ol' human suffering – interspersed with moments of joy, of course – kept calling me to seek within. Unplanned pregancancy and post-natal depression which lingered till after baby number two arrived – followed by the double-wammy of marital breakdown and a dignosis of moderate-to-severe autism in my youngest son – left me on my knees crying for mercy.

Our wounds can be gateways to our souls. I regularly receive spiritual advice to help me overcome suffering, renew my strength and endurance, and keep my soul open to serenity. This advice comes to me through friends, healers, books and synchronicities. I also receive guidance from what I perceive as spirits and from my higher self, or what some people call God.

I'm learning to ask for help when I need it, from both the visible and the invisible worlds. I'm learning the attitude of gratitude and to see beauty everywhere. I'm learning to cast the burden on the spirit within to give my poor rattled mind a break. I'm learning to exist in the moment and accept what is, whilst projecting positive intentions without attachment to results. In this way, I'm learning to magically shape my life. Books that have helped include *The Seven Spiritual Laws Of Success* by Deepak Chopra, *The Game Of Life And How To Play It* by Florence Scovel-Shinn and *The Power Of Now* by Eckhart Tolle.

As the mother of a 'mentally disabled' autistic boy, despair, exhaustion and stress are never far away. But when they threaten to overwhelm, life quickly advises me to ground myself anew in what I perceive as divine energy. On one side I do this through meditation, yoga, love for my children and deep friendships. And on the flipside I honour the hedonist in me via bouts of bawdy laughter, rampant socialising, ecstatic dancing, runaway sensuality and raucous fun. 'Let joy be unconfined!' is my favourite insight.

3

Advice on Babies

Beware the official advice on babies. It's never based on your baby. That's the first reason. The second reason is that it never lasts. Hang about a bit and this year's dead-on bible of baby-rearing becomes next year's refuted orthodoxy.

Read baby books from the middle of the twentieth century, and you get the impression that mothers and fathers were put on this earth to cope with the evil manipulative habits of nasty babies. Babies, as portrayed in these books, are undisciplined drunken abusers just waiting to happen. They know, is the theme. They know how weak you, the parent, are. They'll cry and cry. Deliberately. (Well, it's difficult to cry accidentally, although the wife of one prominent politician recently confessed to me that she was his biggest asset because she was so easily reduced to tears. Put her at the funeral of someone she's met once twenty years ago and she still leaves the church with a satisfactorily-swollen face and fire-brigade-red eyes. The bereaved families love her.)

The old baby books tried to stiffen parents against the too-clever plotting of the miniature adults in the cot. They shouldn't be lifted when they cried; they'd know they had you where they wanted you. They shouldn't be fed on demand; they'd want mealtimes all day and night. Treat them as the enemy, put them in a soft warm prison and take no nonsense from them. Those were the key themes.

Mercifully, later books about babies observed these small creatures as if they were almost human. But only almost. They still had to be trained. Like pets.

Then came a bundle of books which basically said adults know nothing, babies know everything, so just watch yours and listen to it and all will be well. The problem is that those books come with indexes, and the indexes alone are terrifying, because they major on what can go wrong, ranging from cradle cap to meningitis. Plus, they never give you the really clever advice, like the tip I got once from a paediatrician for a radio programme. In the maternity hospital he took me into a room with six babies in cots. One of them was bawling its head off.

'Now, watch,' the doctor said, lifting the wailing child and the blanket around it.

Holding the baby one-armed, he captured its flailing arms with the other and pinned them, gently but firmly, to the baby's chest. Then he folded the blanket around the baby so the child's arms were held in place. Then he held the swaddled baby. Didn't do anything else. Just held it. After a few seconds, the baby's cries died down to nothing.

'Babies get frightened by their own arms,' the paediatrician said, putting the infant back in the cot. 'They've no idea what they are. Restrain their arms gently and they'll usually stop crying. That's why older habits like swaddling – and like the Native American papoose – worked. They kept the baby nice and snug and prevented it being scared by these frantically waving things.'

The best advice I got, just before my only son was born, came – oddly – from a Professor of Business Studies in Trinity College Dublin. Geoffrey McKechnie listened to me blithering on about getting everything right for the impending challenge and then quietly delivered himself of an inescapable truth. 'The great thing about babies,' he pointed out, 'is that they have no precedent.'

Everybody in the room stopped and tried to work this out.

'They don't know what's the proper way to handle them,' Geoff explained. 'They don't know anything. So they don't know if you do it wrong. Or do it in a way the books don't approve.'

It was like getting out of gaol. When our son was born, we put him to sleep in a drawer, because it seemed the right size. He didn't know he was being short-changed.

I breastfed him. No, hold the praise. I breastfed him because breastfeeding is the slob's option. You don't have to invest in bottle-steamers and sterilisers and little tongs for fitting teats on to bottles. You don't have to worry about measuring precisely the right amount. You just plug the baby in. It knows what to do and – except in a minority of cases – it gets on with it.

The man in my life did the colic bit. The baby, for the first four months, took the house down for an hour and a half each evening. He screamed loud enough to be heard in Mozambique. Not long after he'd start, his father would arrive in from work, pick him up and walk the house with him, murmuring admiration for how loud his son could yell. Eventually, in order to hear the murmurs, the baby would lower the volume to a dull roar and then fall asleep on the shoulder that happily presented itself.

Other than the colic period, this was one easygoing baby. Not just easygoing, but fast-developing. At least a month before the books said he should roll over, he – mindful, no doubt, of Professor McKechnie's dictum – decided not to wait. The problem was that he was on our bed at the time, so he rolled over and down. Down onto a hard wood floor. Do you know that horrific silence, lasting several seconds, before a baby realises just how badly he's hurt? During that silence, I had him off the floor, and was halfway down the stairs before he released a lungful of air in a mega-protest.

I took him straight to our local GP. David Chapman opened the door himself, took the baby from me, and leaned close to me in order to hear what I was telling him over the child's bellowing. Then he laid the child down on the examination bed, and, talking quietly to him about how startling the collision with the floor must have been, poked and probed for a bit. The protests reduced to a hiccupping whimper and the whimperer was handed back to its apologetic mother.

'Babies are like drunks,' David said comfortably. 'They never know what's coming, so when they fall, they fall in a completely relaxed way. They're like rubber balls. They do themselves much less damage than older children do as a result.'

I headed for the door of the surgery.

'And they learn from every fall,' the doctor added.

The silently sobbing baby looked at him over my shoulder.

'You've learned just how hard a wooden floor is, haven't you?' David asked him.

A sound like a moan came out of the child by way of confirmation.

'Imagine you teaching yourself that,' David said to him. 'Aren't you just fantastic?'

Kate Hudson, actor
I got so much advice; I just started tuning it out. If one more person told me what I had to do when the baby comes, I was going to shoot 'em.

Harry Robin, author
Every baby needs a lap.

Alan Crosbie, Chairman, Thomas Crosbie Holdings
When we had our first child, Mary got a bit of advice from a friend who herself was a mother, which turned out to be very helpful. 'Let your mind go to mush,' she said. 'Don't fight it. Enjoy the kids. Your normal intelligence will come back, later.'

Steve Doocy, TV host and author
You can never go wrong naming a kid after a family member. Unless that family member is Sammy 'the Bull' Gravano. Short names are less likely to get butchered. If you think you need extra credit on your account to assure you'll get into heaven, you can't go wrong with a saint's name.

Barbara Kingsolver, author
It kills you to see them grow up. But I guess it would kill you quicker if they didn't.

P.J. O'Rourke, author
Getting down on all fours and imitating a rhinoceros stops babies from crying. (Put an empty cigarette pack on your nose for a horn and make loud 'snort' noises.) I don't know why parents don't do this more often. Usually it makes the kid laugh. Sometimes it sends him into shock. Either way it quiets him down. If you're a parent, acting like a rhino has another advantage. Keep it up until the kid is a teenager and he definitely won't have his friends hanging around your house all the time.

H. Jackson Brown, Jr., author
Always kiss your children goodnight – even if they're already asleep.

Bunny Carr, communications expert
When a child is at that boring stage before they can talk or walk – but can sit up – prop them up, put a spoonful of jam or honey into the palm of one

of their hands and put a feather in the other. The feather will stick to the jam and go from hand to hand and the baby can have a good lick at the sweet stuff every now and then. There's a good hour's peace in a spoonful of jam and a feather.

Oldie but goodie…

In 1748, the author of *Dialogues on the Passions, Habits, and Affections Peculiar to Children* advised parents: 'You must create little errands, as if by accident, to send him in the dark, but such as can take up but little time, and increase the length of time by degrees, as you find his courage increase.'

Frederic Leboyer, obstetrician

Being touched and caressed, being massaged, is food for the infant; food as necessary as minerals, vitamins, and proteins. Deprived of this food, the name of which is love, babies would rather die. And often they do.

Mary Hosty, novelist and teacher

A piece of advice my mother-in-law offered has always stuck with me because it is so profound and simple at the same time: 'There are two things you should never take from a child without asking: the first is a sweet. The second is a kiss.' It's a reminder to respect the individuality and autonomy of our children.

4

Advice about Teenagers

'What is happening to our young people? They disrespect their elders, they disobey their parents. They ignore the laws. They riot in the streets inflamed with wild notions. Their morals are decaying…' It could be a comment on *Liveline*, if the language was updated a bit. In fact, it was written two thousand four hundred years ago by Plato, appalled by the teenagers of his time.

A little later Plato's disciple Aristotle addressed the same problem and came up with an explanation for why teenagers were so obnoxious:

> Young people have exalted notions, because they have not yet been humbled by life or learned its necessary limitations; moreover, their hopeful disposition makes them think themselves equal to great things. They would always rather do noble deeds than useful ones; their lives are regulated more by moral feelings than by reasoning – all their mistakes are in the direction of doing things excessively and vehemently. They overdo everything – they love too much; hate too much; and the same with everything else.

Some things never change, and the hormones-on-the-hoof horror of adolescence is one of life's most daunting challenges. One of the great advantages of not being able to see into the future is that, as you hold your beautiful baby, or are entertained by your bubbling toddler, you have no idea what they'll be like ten or fifteen years hence. Roger Ascham, a sixteenth-century scholar, described the years between seventeen and twenty-seven as 'the most dangerous of all in a man's life'. And that was long before speedy cars and crack cocaine.

An underestimated danger in those years lies in the desire of parents to silence, belt or do in their beloved offspring because of the challenge posed by the teenage state. Now, if you're going to kill your teenage son – and it's a possibility many parents examine with some relish – your weapon of choice should not be a ladder. Trust me on this. I tried to decapitate my own son using a wooden ladder so heavy that getting it off the ground was something of an achievement. I kept this a secret for many years, divulging it in a confessional blurt to a gentle, warm, successful full-time mother of five. I expected her to be horrified.

'Well, the thing is, you use whatever's handy,' she told me. 'You can't plan properly with a teenager. I lost it with our eldest and the nearest weapon was the sweeping brush. I swear to God, I nearly broke his legs with it.'

The important point here is that your teenage son or daughter does not have to be shooting drugs, mitching from school, wrecking the house with cider parties any time you leave it in order for a conviction to build up on your side that no young person was ever so poisonously, personally venomous and vile. It's a process you have to go through, like teenage acne, only later, when you're tireder.

The really maddening thing is when your partner doesn't go through that process, but stays tight with the kid when it's perfectly clear to all reasonable people that this kid no longer belongs in the human race and should be put on a small island and made eat periwinkles until they admit their crimes and make a firm purpose of amendment. The man in my life used to treat the conflicts between his wife and son the way you'd treat something inexplicable but disgusting, like a strange goat crapping on the couch. He himself just did unconditional love (punctuated by a half-yearly rant which was as entertaining as it was surprising) and wanted me to do the same. Unconditional love I wasn't good at, so when the phone rang one night after a battle, I found it difficult to muster up a cheery 'Howya.'

The caller was Máire Geoghegan-Quinn, then Minister for Justice. She figured out quickly what was up with me.

'Oh, nobody told you,' she said comfortably.

'Nobody told me what?'

'Nobody told you that when your kid is about fifteen or sixteen, they take them away and replace them with a lookalike that's an absolute swine. Horrible, contemptuous, filthy, disagreeable, untrustworthy swine. But, you know the good part? When the kid is about twenty or twenty-one, they do another swap and you get your own child back as nice as they used to be. Trust me.'

It made no sense at all, and it made perfect sense. The notion of having a teenage changeling who would eventually be removed was weirdly helpful. She was wrong in only one thing. The adult son who replaced the changeling was even better than the pre-teen version.

While most parents who seek advice about how to help (or not kill) their teenagers tend to ask friends and family, some seek it further afield. Possibly because the Nobel Prizewinning physicist, Richard Feynman, had a genius for making the complex simple, a man named Vincent Van Der Hyde wrote to him, having read one of his populist science books, asking for advice about his stepson, who was then sixteen years old:

> Here is this kid, bright, very good in math and chemistry and physics. Flying radio controlled model airplanes, and reading books about wing design that have a lot of equations in them that I'm sure I don't know how to solve.
>
> But at the same time he's trying to grow up and figure himself and his world out a little. A bit overweight, a little shy, not a whole lot of self-confidence. So he makes up for it by coming on a little strong, playing macho sometimes.

While not wanting, as he put it, to be a pushy parent, Van Der Hyde was bothered by a pattern the teenager's teachers had observed over two years:

> It seems that he picks all the science up fast, sees how you do a thing, and then he wants to go on as fast as he can on his own. Some of the teachers really encourage that, which is great. But...it turns out that everybody grades on the basis of how you score on the tests, and the tests only cover what they teach to everybody. Marvin, that's his name, sees the basic stuff as to easy for him and hence it's beneath him to hand in the routine day-to-day assignments...so his grades are down. That, of course, is a bummer.

The man writing the letter and the teenager both, he went on, loved a particular book, which was funny, informative – and written by a Nobel Prizewinner: Feynman. 'Now, you obviously know a lot about science,' the letter writer went on, 'and if the book is any indication you know a lot about how people work too. And who knows what it is that would make a smart sixteen-year-old stop for a minute and think about what it is he really wants in his life (at least for a while) and what it is going to take to get it.'

The stepfather asked Feynman to write to him, pointing out: 'Just knowing that somebody "out there" understands and cares a little can make a big difference sometimes. It helps keep the wings straight and the nose up.'

Feynman responded within a week, with a kind and lengthy letter of advice, in which he said, *inter alia*:

> For some people (for me, and, I suspect, for your son) when you are young you only want to go as fast as far and as deep as you can in one subject – all the others are neglected as being relatively uninteresting.
>
> But later on when you get older you find nearly everything is really interesting if you go into it deeply enough. Because what you learned as a youth was that some one thing is more interesting as you go deeper. Only later do you find it true of other things – ultimately everything too. Let him go, let him get all distorted studying what interests him the most as much as he wants. True, our school system will grade him poorly – but he will make out. Far better than knowing only a little about a lot of things.
>
> It may encourage you to know that the parents of the Nobel prizewinner Don Glaser (physicist inventor of the bubble chamber) were advised, when their son was in the third grade, that he should be

transferred to a school for retarded children. The parents stood firm and were vindicated in the fourth grade when their son turned out to be a whiz at long division. Don tells me he remembers he didn't bother to answer any of the dumb obvious questions of the earlier grades – but he found long division a little harder, the answers not obvious, and the process fascinating so began to pay attention,

So don't worry – but don't let him get too much out of hand like Don Glaser. What advice can I give him? He won't take it, of course. But the two of you – father and son – should take walks in the evening and talk (without purpose or routes) about this and that. Because his father is a wise man, and the son I think is wise too for they have the same opinions I had when I was a father and when I was a son too. These don't exactly agree, of course, but the deeper vision of the older man will grow out of the concentrated energetic attention of the younger. Patience.

Q: What do you have to do to train yourself to be whatever it is you want to be?

A: There are many roads all different that have been taken by many different scientists. The road I took is the one your son takes – work as hard and as much as you want to on the things you like to do the best. Try to keep the other grades from going zero if you can. Don't think of what 'you want to be,' but what you 'want to do'. Luckily he knows that already, so let him do it. (But keep up some kind of a minimum with other things so that society doesn't stop you from doing anything at all.)

Q: What is it that would make a smart sixteen-year-old stop for a minute and think...'

A: Nothing, now, I hope. But to fall in love with a wonderful woman, and to talk to her quietly in the night will do wonders.

Stop worrying, Papa. Your kid is wonderful. Yours from another Papa of another wonderful kid. Sincerely

Richard P. Feynman

When Feynman's daughter, Michelle, was assembling her father's letters into a collection for publication many years later (*Perfectly Reasonable Deviations from the Beaten Track*: *The Letters of Richard P. Feynman, 2005*), she found that the sixteen-year-old had met a wonderful woman – when he was in college – had married her and was now himself the father of two children, as well as being in the final year of a PhD in physical oceanography.

'My son has never forgotten,' his father told Feynman's daughter, 'how one of the "greats" took a few minutes just for him...'

Jo O'Donoghue, publisher

One of the best bits of advice I've ever got is that when you ask someone to do something they are entitled to refuse. Just as you are entitled to refuse to do something for them. Might sound obvious but I've spent a lot of my life expecting people to oblige me just because they're my children (they should: it's their house too), my friend (look at all I do for her), my colleague (I recommended him for promotion, damn him). This realisation has contributed immeasurably to harmony in my home, which contains two teenagers and a dog. And guess what: the less you invest in expecting people to do things just because you ask them, the more they're likely to come to your assistance when they see you need it.

5

ADVICE TO TEENAGERS

Here's a suggestion. Let's have a moratorium on advice to teenagers. They're up to here in it. They get it from their parents. Their teachers. Their sports coaches. Their websites. Their magazines. Their friends. Their enemies.

They get advice on how to study, what to eat, when and how to have sex or not have sex, what to wear and how much time to spend at any of the above. Teenagers may have more money and more options than they ever had, but they move through this hormone-sodden period of their lives through a fog of advice. Inevitably, little of the advice sticks. But even its failure to stick causes problems, irritating the teenager and (by its lack of results) infuriating parents and teachers.

The only good thing about what teenagers get, as opposed to what happens to younger children, is that at least it qualifies as advice, whereas everybody gives orders to younger children: Eat up your porridge. Don't stare. Tidy your room. Leave that alone. Don't put that in your mouth. Don't make me come down there.

When it comes to advice, most teenagers, fortunately, have an overdeveloped immune system. Advise them not to wear such a short skirt or such a midriff-exposing top and they'll sulk, go back upstairs, change – and bring the mini-skirt and the minier top with them to change into later. Advise them not to drink, and they'll have a party in the house the minute you go off for that long weekend. Advise them to eat a balanced diet and they'll spend hours on the Web in their room finding out the latest anorectic tricks.

According to psychologist Judith Rich Harris, teenagers don't pay any attention to parental or grandparental or other advice because their peers have much more influence on their attitudes and behaviours than do their progenitors. Her theory goes like this. If two parents from China, France or Korea immigrate to Ireland, and have children in Ireland, what language will the children speak? English. Will they speak it better than their parents ever will? Of course. What accent will their English have? Dublin. (Unless they're being brought up in Cork or Roscrea, in which case those are the twangs they'll have.) Bottom line: parents believe themselves to be hugely important in the formation of the adults their kids become, but aren't. What's even more dispiriting (if you're a parent) is that while you may believe your advice was what made your twenty-year-old turn out to be quite like you, it was the shared DNA that really did it. Genetics are more important than most parents want to believe. Nature knocks hell out of nurture.

That doesn't stop parents issuing advice to their offspring. But any teenager today who harbours a desire to belt their old dear with a brick should hold off. No matter how big an advice-monger their mother or father may be, they're not at the races by comparison with Lord Chesterfield.

Philip-Dormer Stanhope, Earl of Chesterfield, was born in 1694. He became an MP, an ambassador and eventually Lord-Lieutenant of Ireland. None of which is why he is remembered, today. He's remembered today because of his advice to his son. He gave more advice to his son than any son could reasonably expect. From the time the son was seven, Dad sent him letters on the *Art of*

Becoming a Man of the World and a Gentleman.

Chesterfield's stunningly-erudite flow of letters was motivated, he told his son, by the father's desire to get him up to speed: to make sure the boy did everything at the right age, especially those things his father should have done and didn't. He pointed out – sensibly and (as he would put it) sillily, that if he'd done his learning young, he'd have copped on to many things easily which were much harder for him to cop on to when he was older. The silly part of this theory is his ignoring of the fact that every individual has to make their own mistakes. Chesterfield wrote:

> Save yourself now, then, I beg of you, that regret and trouble hereafter. Ask questions, and many questions; and leave nothing till you are thoroughly informed of it. Such pertinent questions are far from being illbred or troublesome to those of whom you ask them; on the contrary, they are a tacit compliment to their knowledge; and people have a better opinion of a young man, when they see him desirous to be informed.

He had a point. The problem, with Chesterfield, was that he had several thousand points, whether related to negotiation skills, curing illness or getting along with unpleasant people. Or time management: 'Whatever business you have, do it the first moment you can; never by halves, but finish it without interruption, if possible. Business must not be sauntered and trifled with.'

Lord Chesterfield was a widely-read and highly cultivated man (although Samuel Johnson thought he was a well-mannered nonentity whose praise wasn't worth having) who loved books and music and did his dogmatic best to get his son into the same habits. But his recurring theme was getting along with people. Some of his letters could have been written by Dale Carnegie, stressing, as they do, that the way to win friends and influence people is by paying attention to the other person, rather than oneself:

> There is nothing so brutally shocking, nor so little forgiven, as a seeming inattention to the person who is speaking to you. I have known many a man knocked down, for (in my opinion) a much lighter provocation, than that shocking inattention which I mean. I have seen many people, who, while you are speaking to them, instead of looking at, and attending to you, fix their eyes upon the ceiling or some other part of the room, look out of the window, play with a dog, twirl their snuff-box, or pick their nose. Nothing discovers a little, futile, frivolous mind more than this, and nothing is so offensively ill-bred; it is an explicit declaration on your part, that every the most trifling object, deserves your attention more than all that can be said by the person who is speaking to you. Judge of the sentiments of hatred and resentment, which such treatment must excite in every breast where any degree of self-love dwells; you must be extremely well-bred and polite, but without the troublesome forms and stiffness of ceremony. You must be respectful and assenting, but without being servile and abject.
>
> You must be frank, but without indiscretion; and close, without being costive. You must keep up dignity of character, without the least pride of birth or rank. You must be gay within all the bounds of decency and respect; and grave without the affectation of

> wisdom, which does not become the age of twenty.
> You must be essentially secret, without being dark
> and mysterious. You must be firm, and even bold, but
> with great seeming modesty.

Updated a bit, that's not far from what many parents would advise
their twenty-first-century children to be. Unfortunately, the end
result of all this advice was a tad disappointing. The son, a stubby,
stout little lad, did his best. He tried, God love him, he tried. He
read all the letters with which his father inundated him, and bore
the paternal criticisms of his own responses as 'infrequent and
laconic'. He became an MP. Briefly. Unsuccessfully. Then he went
and snuffed it at an early age, leaving a ticking time-bomb for his
father, as Virginia Woolf noted:

> He left it to his widow to break the news which he had
> lacked the heart or the courage to tell his father—that
> he had been married all these years to a lady of low
> birth, who had borne him children. The Earl took the
> blow like a gentleman. His letter to his daughter-in-law
> is a model of urbanity. He began the education of his
> grandsons.

Another generation to be lined up and subjected to the old Earl's
pearls of wisdom. Even better, a generation disadvantaged by the
'low birth' of their mother.

On the other hand, that very low birth may have helped the
advice-immunity of the grandchildren, since they don't seem to
have kept any letters from their grandfather, who is inarguably the
most relentless advice-giver in the history of family life.

The best form of parental advice to teenagers isn't verbal.

It's example. There's not much point in parents who take several alcoholic drinks each night advising their kids to stay off the booze. Statistics suggest that most kids who drink to excess get started – and in many cases, continue to get their supplies – at home. Leaving your children unhectored while living the values and demonstrating the viability of the behaviours you would like them to adopt is not a bad approach. Especially if it's informed by unconditional love, so that when they make a bad mistake or do something of which they are ashamed, they still regard their parents as the best people to tell.

Whether you are a parent or a teacher of teenagers, do not kid yourself that learning the words of the latest song or coming out with what you perceive to be 'cool' slang will make you part of their group. It won't and it shouldn't. You're an adult. Behave like one – and let them behave as teenagers do. Because no matter how many cool phrases you learn, you still belong to a different generation and trying to convince younger people that older people did everything they do is a pointless exercise, partly because some of the things teenagers do today, people even as little as ten years older didn't do at their age, notably put their profiles up on Bebo or MySpace.

Now, here's an area where a little advice in the form of a longevity warning is no harm. Material uploaded to the Web lasts longer than forever. Even if the original site gets taken down, anybody who downloaded material from it can continue to circulate it. So videos of a teenager having sex, flashing, taking drugs or throwing up after taking drugs or alcohol can have long-term consequences. Increasingly, employers are Googling the names of potential employees, and the evidence is mounting that many job offers get shelved when the employer finds something on the web which makes the potential employee appear to be rather less than a great find.

Noel Dempsey, TD, Minister for Transport and Communications
I was rather hot-headed as a youngster, always getting myself into rows on the football or hurling field when I was at school. I remember getting a belt of a hurley at some stage, and going bald-headed to kill the fella who had hit me. The teacher grabbed me by the two arms and just held me there, pinned, while I wriggled and squiggled, trying to escape and get on with doing damage to the other player.

'You have to learn one thing,' the teacher said, very quietly, while holding me still. 'You have to control that temper of yours, or it'll control you. Now, I'm going to count to ten while you make that decision – one, two, three – now, remember, for the rest of your life, you have to be in control of it – four, five, six – or it's going to be in control of you – seven, eight...'

It probably took him a whole minute to count to ten, and by the time he'd got there, I'd cooled down enough not to head off to kill the other fella. The phrase stuck with me ever since: You've got to control your temper, or it'll control you...

Harry Truman
I have found the best way to give advice to your children is to find out what they want and then advise them to do it.

Dermod Moore, author
The best advice I ever got was during my tumultuous adolescence. I was like a horse repeatedly refusing a fence when it came to working for the Leaving Certificate. In my punk-influenced outlaw eyes, the system was corrupt. I had no desire to conform, saw no reasonable incentive to do so, was frightened of failure (I had gained five As in the Inter, the year before) and the ethos of my school was claustrophobically focused on a bourgeois mediocrity. In the constant arguments with my parents and headmaster, I could see no way out. It was profoundly depressing.

One day I came home to find this advice typed out on a piece of card, sellotaped to a leaf of the Swiss cheese plant in my bedroom. My mother had left it there. It was taken from the preface to Doris Lessing's novel *The Golden Notebook* and went as follows:

> You are in the process of being indoctrinated. What you are being taught is an amalgam of current prejudice and the choices of this particular culture. The slightest look at history will show you how impermanent these must be. You are being taught by people who have been able to accommodate themselves to a regime of thought laid down by their predecessors. Those of you who are more robust and individual than others, will be encouraged to leave and find ways of educating yourself – educating your own judgement. Those that stay must remember, always and all the time, that they are being moulded and patterned to fit into the narrow and particular needs of this society.

Concerning the pressing issue of whether I'd knuckle down and do some work for the exams, the advice was spectacularly unhelpful. I learned it off by rote and started parotting it back to my mother, who rightly complained that I was missing the point. But, in retrospect, I don't think anything would have helped me at the time. I ended up wasting two years, flunking the Leaving completely. At the age of nineteen, I was working as a dishwasher in a restaurant. But then I got a place in drama school, and things began to click into place.

The older I get, the more relevant this advice has become, and it deeply underpins my philosophy, my writing, and in particular my teaching and psychotherapy practice. Irish society is particularly sophisticated in the way it moulds and patterns individuals, and I spend a large part of my life, in some way or another, deconstructing that patterning and encouraging people to educate their own judgement and follow their own light. Would I have done so without reading it? Most probably. But is there a more concise or relevant way of communicating this message? I doubt it.

Paddy McDermott, CEO, Transitions Optical

The best advice I ever got at that age was from my mother. 'If you try to create an impression,' she used to say, 'that's the impression you create.'

Ian Elliott, Chief Executive Officer, Catholic Church's National Board for Child Protection

It is only with the benefit of hindsight that I am able to determine the best advice that I have ever received. It was from my father who was passing on to me advice he had received from his father. (I am not sure about preceding generations but it probably applies to them too.) The advice was simply this. 'Don't be limited by other people's expectations of who they think you are. Be who you are and use life as a means of discovering who you can become.'

This connected with me as a shy, quiet, and insecure adolescent growing up in the Dublin of the fifties and sixties. I found it liberating to realise that many of my inhibitions were self-imposed and were really under my control. I took it as an invitation to take control of my life rather than letting it be shaped by others, and I have never forgotten that.

Albert Ellis, psychotherapist

Some of us walk around all day long getting on our own cases: 'I've got to do this. I've got to do that. I should have said this to that person. I need to be more that. I ought to be more organised. I should be more attractive, intelligent, witty, popular and personable. I ought to be more assertive. I need to be less aggressive. I've got to speak up more. I really need to keep my mouth shut...' Some of us 'should on ourselves' all day long!

Tracy Brennan, Trace Literary Agency, Indiana

I think the best advice I ever got, I received from my grandmother who I absolutely loved. Aside from telling me to be kind, good, respectful and gracious – which many times I was not – she also told me not to take for granted those you care about and don't miss out on telling them how you feel.

I didn't always listen to her advice. I was busy being a teenager and like most other teens thought I knew everything and was full of wisdom. Oh to know then, what I know now!! There were some missed opportunities for me and I still regret my actions.

One was with my father. I guess I couldn't get past the anger I felt for him and his alcoholism. I just wished he could be like my other friend's fathers. I now realise I was too busy looking at all the bad things and forgot to see the good in him. He died when I was away at college. I wish now that I spent more time talking to him and trying to understand what he was going through and why he chose to do what he did.

Another was with a friend of mine. Betsy. A dear person, but a very high-maintenance friend, nonetheless. She could be very demanding and let's just say had a lot of issues, alcohol and drug abuse to name a few. But deep down she had a heart of gold. She always wanted to be someone she was not, ranging from looks to material things. She lost several friends along the way due to her demanding nature. I just kind of removed myself from her circle. She reached out to me on a couple of occasions, and I wish I had responded differently. She took a great job offer in Cleveland, Ohio and we lost touch, but I'd think of her often and wonder how she was doing, especially being in a completely new circle of friends and co-workers and ones who didn't know her past. We'd write at Christmas and I'd see her once in a blue moon when she'd come back to Indiana to visit.

I received a message from her former live-in/boyfriend – who was always there for her despite her flaws. The call came while we were on vacation, so I was unable to respond right away. He called to let me know that Betsy was in the hospital in Cleveland. She was septic, had pneumonia and was on life support and things looked grim. Then there was another call about three days later letting me know that she had died. It really shocked me to my core. And it really ate me up knowing she died such a lonely person. Another missed opportunity for me.

As I've grown older, and hopefully wiser, I definitely try to follow Gram's advice as best I can.

Sean Gallagher, Managing Director, SmartHomes

I had a major visual impairment when I was a child, so, because I could only see words and not full sentences, I read slowly and awkwardly. The teachers assumed, not that I was visually impaired, but that I just wasn't bright. For a time I was put in a sort of 'dunce's' corner. When you are treated differently, you begin to feel different.

I was lucky that when I reached sixth class, the headmaster of my primary school, Tom Gawley, pulled me aside after a drama class. He was himself an artist who probably felt as misunderstood and different as I felt at the time. He told me that it was OK to dream. He told me that I had talents I didn't know about and that the only thing I was missing was the confidence to follow them.

'You may not take the same path other people take,' he told me. 'You need to find, or create, your own path. Life is not about having and getting, it is about being and becoming. You can do anything you want to do and be anything you want to be, so long as you can dream it. If you can dream it, you can become it.'

That advice stayed with me and helped me right throughout my life.

6

ADVICE ON LOVE

In any office, in any group of 'les girls' or in any family, when it comes to giving advice on love, bitten tongues abound. And rightly so. Anyone feeling the urge to give advice to another on who to fall in love with or who to leave should count to ten. Ten times. And then have second thoughts. Because nobody understands your particular relationship the way you do. What you see depends on where you stand, and outsiders always get a view of a relationship unrelated to, and sometimes in radical contrast to, the view held by the couple themselves.

Before we ever became a couple, the man in my life suggested a strategy in this regard:

> We will have fights. Everybody does. When we have a fight, don't tell your mother about it. Because we will make up. We'll sort it so our relationship is even stronger as a result of the fight. But your mother won't be around when we're doing that, so she'll always be left with a shadowed version of our relationship.

The urge to get sympathy when you have a fight with the person you love often does damage to the relationship you have with other people. You vomit forth your misery. The other person listens and forgets. If they're wise. Maybe one per cent of friends can do this. The other ninety-nine a) don't forget, b) get partisan, c) start sticking their spoon in your pudding by offering advice.

They tell you what you're entitled to. (In love, there are no entitlements.) They tell you what to tell your partner. (Imported speeches never ring true in relationships.) They tell you to leave. (Sometimes, particularly if violence is involved, they're right. But if you don't take their advice, they get mad at you and you feel got at from both sides.) They tell you what they did in similar circumstances. (There are no similar circumstances – every unhappy couple is unhappy in its own way.) They explain the processes going on behind the battle. (Which is a bit like a meteorologist explaining lousy summer weather: marginally interesting, but doesn't solve the problem of what you're going to do with the kids the sixth day of unremitting rain.)

'Don't ask, don't tell' is not a bad way to approach advice-seeking about love. Other people mean well, but that doesn't imply they can hand you an externally-developed solution for your problem.

Advice on relationships tends to be rational. Falling in love tends to be irrational. Ergo, rarely do the twain productively meet. Robert Graves summed it up in a puzzled question:

> Why have such scores of lovely, gifted girls
> Married such impossible men?
> Simple self-sacrifice may be ruled out,
> And missionary endeavour, nine times out of ten.

Friends and relatives who propose that you make two lists about your prospective life partner, one showing the positives, the other the negatives, need to be told to get a grip. I've known individuals who did this, to sort out their minds when they have fallen for someone over whom questions hang. I've never seen it work. And if I were the prospective partner and found I had been opted for after an arithmetical exercise about the pros and cons of moving in with me, the carpet would have scorch-marks, I'd be out of there *so* fast.

When I reached the stage of 'going out with' men, my mother, as mothers do, gave me multiple bits of advice. I think she thought I was in much more demand than I actually was, because one day, standing at the sink, she produced a *non sequitur* which floored me.

'You may be sleeping with people,' she announced. 'That's your business. Just, if you are, don't tell me. I don't want to know and you don't want to hear the reaction I would have.'

I wasn't, as it happened. Not because I was chaste, but because I was unchased. No man, up to that point – I was in my early twenties – had given my virtue much of a run for its money. But I got the message and it made sense. Mothers, back then, didn't do Linsdey Lohan/Lisa Lohan partying together.

Another piece of advice she gave, which made sense but which nobody ever imagines applies to them, was to quote the New Testament (Luke 23:31): 'If they do these things in the green wood, what will they do in the dry?' The inference to be drawn is that if your lover, in the early ecstasy of the relationship, is cheap or smart at your expense or unfaithful or unpunctual or boringly self-absorbed, the chances are that this trait will worsen after you marry them, not improve. A.E.Housman put it this way:

> Oh, when I was in love with you,
> Then I was clean and brave,
> And miles around the wonder grew
> How well did I behave.

Ma was strong on financial independence for women, long before it became a given in Irish society. Earn and own your own money was a recurring theme. Earn and own your own money no matter how generous he is. Earn and own your own money before, during and after you have children. It gives a solid foundation for any decisions you make in problematical situations. You're not trapped in a rotten relationship for financial reasons. She was and is right. The impoverishment of women is too often a consequence of relationship break-ups.

The best maternal advice I got on love, however, wasn't even cast as advice, more as a reflective observation.

'At the end of your life,' she once said, 'when you look back on your marriage, it's not the great moments of pain or passion you remember. It's the great moments of fun…'

Katherine Hepburn, *actor*
If you want to sacrifice the admiration of many men for the criticism of one, go ahead, get married.

Alan Crosbie, *Chairman, Thomas Crosbie Holdings*
I once asked a friend who was part of a really great couple with a fantastic marriage what their secret was.
'We talk a lot,' she told me. 'And we make love a lot.'

Linda Cullen, *Head of Television, CoCo Television*
One of the best pieces of advice I ever got was from my mother. It was about my former partner, who had left me.

'Do you think she'll come back, Mum?' I kept asking her.

She'd hold my hand and very kindly say, 'No pet, she won't.' The reason it was great advice was that I knew Mum loved me more than anyone in the world so she had no agenda other than my recovery. And she said it every time I asked, which must have been so hard; she must have wanted to give me hope but loved me too much to do that and took it on the chin when I got annoyed or cried or went silent. It doesn't sound like advice, but it was.

'She's not coming back, lick your wounds, I'm always here for you, try to get on with it,' was the advice, all of it hidden inside 'No pet, she won't.'

Woody Allen, film director
Sex without love is a meaningless experience, but as far as meaningless experiences go it's pretty damn good.

Letty Cottin Pogrebin, author
The best advice I ever got was, 'You don't have to do anything now.' These words probably strike you as tepid and innocuous but to me they were profound because they were exactly what I needed to hear in 1962.

Back story: I had just broken up with Fred, an intense young man who kept insisting I should marry him even though I didn't love him. Given his devotion, I was careful to formulate my parting words in the most gentle possible terms. Nevertheless, Fred promptly repaired to the men's room of a pub in Greenwich Village and slashed his wrists. Though he did not succeed at doing away with himself, he did end up in St. Vincent's hospital with police and doctors in attendance, and he gave my name as the person to be contacted in an emergency.

The phone call from the cops totally freaked me out. I see myself as a rescuer, not a femme fatale who leaves jilted suitors to death by razor blade. Clearly his suicide attempt was Fred's bid to get my attention and lure me back. I agonised over what to do? Should I go to the hospital and comfort the poor guy? Take him back now and worry about the marriage proposal later? Call his mother and make clear that Fred's survival was her responsibility from now on? Reprimand Fred for traumatising me but stick with him until he was strong enough to get along without me? Tell him what a manipulative drama queen he was, that his self-destructive ploy was a bust, and then leave him once and for all, even if he jumps off the Brooklyn Bridge and when fished out of the East River gives my name as the person to be contacted in an emergency? Or what?

I was truly at a loss. Didn't want Fred in my life but also didn't want his death on my conscience. When it became clear that I couldn't handle this conundrum alone, a close friend talked me into seeing her psychiatrist, Dr Robert Naiman, to get his advice. (You should know that I was, at the time, deeply suspicious of head doctors. I may well have been the only Jew in Greenwich Village who had not been psychoanalysed or therapised and I was not inclined to break my record.)

'I've tied myself up in knots,' I moaned after outlining the situation to Dr Naiman. 'I've been trying to figure out what to do but I can't. I'm stuck.'

That was when this brilliant, unassuming, incisive psychiatrist said his seven magic words: 'You don't have to do anything now.'

This had never occurred to me. Doing nothing was not among the options I'd ever offered myself when confronted with a dilemma. I'm an activist, a compulsive problem solver with a terminal can-do personality. To me and others similarly afflicted, the thought of not doing anything is a cop-out that we interpret as an admission of personal inadequacy, and the idea of not doing it now is the way of the wimp. What Dr Naiman's simple advice introduced into my arsenal of behaviors was the idea of inaction as an act in itself – and the realisation that doing nothing is, in fact, doing something because it allows the status quo to settle into place. When it settles, you notice either that the troublesome situation has changed of its own accord or that you are able to look at it in a different way than you did when the hot breath of crisis was snorting down your neck.

Taking seriously Dr Naiman's advice, I chose inaction that day, and the day after, and the day after that. When two weeks of 'nows' had gone by without me doing anything and without a word from the cops, the hospital, or Fred, I discovered to my astonishment that I no longer had a problem. Or rather, the problem had solved itself without me. I never heard from Fred again. I assume that he got over me in due course, his wrists healed, and he went on to have a perfectly pleasant life with someone else. Since then, Dr Naiman's seven magic words have helped me countless times to cool down my overheated can-do impulses and remind myself that just because I can act doesn't mean I should or must.

Mother Theresa
Some professors came to our house in Calcutta. 'Tell us something,' one of them said, 'that would change our lives.' And I said, 'Smile at each other.' Then one of them asked me (a strange question): 'Are you married?' 'Yes,' I said. 'And I sometimes find it very difficult to smile at Jesus. He can be so demanding!' And I repeated: 'Smile at each other. Smile at people you live with – it's easy to smile at strangers.'

Adela Rogers St John, author and journalist
I think every woman is entitled to a middle husband she can forget.

Tom Savage, management consultant and former marriage counseller
The minute you hear someone say that they're working on their marriage, you know that marriage is for the high jump. Why? Because any close relationship requires effort, commitment and constant determination to make the other person happy. It's natural. It's directed towards another person. Not a concept. If you are working on your marriage, you shouldn't be. You should be working to make life worthwhile for the person you're married to, not dutifully fulfilling an externally-imposed task. And you sure as hell shouldn't talk about it.

Marcel Proust, author
Like everybody who is not in love, he thought one chose the person to be loved after endless deliberations and on the basis of particular qualities or advantages.

H. Jackson Brown Jr., author
Marry the right person. This one decision will determine 90 per cent of your happiness or misery.

Albert Ellis, psychotherapist
When one mate has strong prejudices in favour or against certain sex practices, the other partner should try to be unusually understanding and uncritical, even if the practices that are favoured or disfavoured seem to be outlandish. If the presumably more reasonable mate will at least give the 'outlandish' procedures an honest try, he or she may find that they are really not as bad as they seem to be.

Tom Savage, management consultant and former marriage counseller
Married life should be a contest of generosities.

Steve Doocey, television host
Affairs are so sad. One day you think you're happily married, next thing you know there's a boiled rabbit in your kitchen stockpot.

Because every marriage has 750,000 moving parts, chances are yours will eventually hit a pothole. Sometimes it knocks your front end out of alignment and you need to get professional help. That's why ministers and priests and marriage counsellers and bartenders are standing by to help you through the rough times.

Padhraic Ó Ciardha, leasphríomhcheannasaí, TG4
'*Ná lig do rún le bun an chlaí go bhféacha tú thar a bharr.*' This was one of
my late mother's favourite proverbs. It translates literally as, 'Don't reveal
your secret (even) to the base of a wall until you see what's on the other
side.' It was her way of telling us to choose our friends carefully and to be
prudent in sharing secrets with people we didn't know well.

Mary Hosty, novelist and teacher
From my mother-in-law came a very important piece of advice. One evening
when we were staying with her, I came back from a shopping trip. We had
just started paying our first mortgage and I hadn't bought anything apart
from Dunnes three-pack cheap tights in six months. I couldn't stand it any
longer. It was spring and the shops were full of pastel-coloured clothes and
elegant white shoes. I bought the shoes and a pale blue skirt and realised
we'd be living on macaroni cheese for the rest of the month. I sat at the
table with husband and in-laws – absolutely rigid with guilt and a certain
amount of resentment that the husband hadn't greeted my purchases with
some show of enthusiasm.

Cáit, my mother-in-law, quickly sized up the situation and drew me
aside after dinner.

'A word of advice, *a ghrá*,' she whispered to me in the corridor. 'Always
deduct thirty per cent.'

I didn't understand.

'Knock thirty per cent off the price of everything you buy. It makes for
a much happier marriage.'

Adi Roche, Founder, Chernobyl Children's Project International
'Grief is the price we pay for love.' Mum on the death of Dad.

7

ADVICE TO WOMEN

Women today are surrounded, and surround themselves with assumptions. Men, ditto. But – with one exception – the assumptions about men don't tend to limit their action the way the assumptions about women limit their actions and progress. The exception is the assumption always made that men are stronger than women, which is true if you want a bed lifted, but not if you measure strength by capacity to survive. Women last longer than men do.

The assumptions around women are different from the assumptions that floated in the intellectual ether about their mothers. They're sure as hell different from the assumptions that circulated around their grandmothers.

Their grandmothers concentrated on getting married. Not on romance. Not on knock-your-socks-off sex. That was because families saw men as the breadwinners. Ergo men had to be educated, and if there was enough money – in those days before free education and CAO forms – girls could be educated, too. If only because when they got married, they'd be able to do a better job raising the kids they had. And, while they were getting educated, they should think about teaching (which would let them get off early enough to be at home with their kids and had long holidays, likewise) nursing (because, hey, women were naturally compassionate and the outfits, particularly those polka-dotted ones in the Adelaide, were cute) and the civil service (because it was permanent and pensionable and if the woman was unfortunate enough to be passed over for marriage and left a spinster, she was set for life).

The following generation got more options. They could be air hostesses, which not only held the exciting prospects of meeting glamorous people while wearing even cuter uniforms than the Adelaide nurses, but led to the possibility of snagging a pilot, than which nothing could be a bigger social coup. They could be PR executives, schmoozing journalists to get mentions for mostly female products into the women's pages of the papers. They could – if they were really lucky – work in TV. Not as newsreaders, mind you. You know yourself: if you had a woman reading the news, it would be too distracting for the viewers. They'd never be able to concentrate on the important information being transmitted.

Roughly thirty years ago, in theory, all the limiting assumptions about women bit the dust. Equality legislation came in. More and more women got to third level, and many of them outperformed men. Sometimes they even outperformed men in areas like law and physics. Worse, they got ambitious. They wanted to stop being Girl Fridays and be bosses.

Every time one of them became a boss of a substantial company, or a county manager or a secretary general in a government department, it was a step forward. To total equality, right?

Wrong. Count the number of civil service secretary generals who are female. Count the number of county managers. If you move into the private sector, count the number of women at the top of substantial operations. Or, better still, name them. Because you probably can: Danuta Gray in Vodafone. Joan Kehoe in Quintillion. Norah Casey in Harmonia.

The reality is that the majority of confident graduate women will not end up in top jobs. Because they get enmeshed in assumptions about them. Not discrimination. Assumptions. Often unspoken. Sometimes, because of equality legislation and the fear of Melanie Pine (Director of the Equality Tribunal), unspeakable. Absolutely unwritable. But there, nonetheless. A bunch of assumptions, any one of which isn't that limiting, but which, when you add them up, are like the little ropes the Lilliputians used to tie Gulliver down: amazingly effective at limiting freedom of movement.

I spend a lot of my professional time advising women when they become aware of the Lilliputian strings represented by their own and other people's assumptions. When they hit a wall and realise it may not be enough to be qualified and competent: that other people assume they should dress in a business uniform and use makeup. When they get promoted and find the transition away from their former female colleagues to higher, more male levels in an organisation more difficult than they expected. When a man swears or tells a dirty joke in a meeting and then apologises – to her, because she's a woman. When she takes extra leave to be with her babies and finds that when she heads back to work, she has lost confidence or other people have moved on and assume she's now mainly into motherhood. When she gets fat and doesn't want to go to the class reunion because she assumes they will decide she has 'let herself go'. When she figures that women who are really successful in business must be hard and must have made unacceptable sacrifices on the home or parenting front to get there.

And the advice?

- Nothing qualifies you for motherhood. It happens to many women. It changes everything. Nobody can tell you in advance. The only advice anybody can give you is: don't underestimate the impact it's going to have

on your life and don't rule out anything. You don't
know until you're there what you'll do.

- Letting other people own a bit of your head is
a mistake. Shaping your life in response to real or
possible criticisms never satisfies the people who
criticise you, and always leaves you unsatisfied and
resentful.

- Do what will make you happy. Don't hope that
someone else will make you happy.

- Don't compare yourself to anybody else.

- Don't hang around with people who pay you most
attention when you're sick or have problems. They
are social necrophiles. Hang around with people who
pay most attention to you when you're trying the
impossible and who want you to be a success, not an
interesting victim.

- Keep your mouth shut. Three people can keep a
secret – if two of them are dead. We've been brought
up to believe that expressing ourselves is good for us.
Not expressing ourselves is often better. Especially
if expressing ourselves takes the form of whinges,
passive-aggressive sighs and pseudo-resigned re-
proaches or bitching.

- Don't buy into bullshit. A seaweed bath or having
your back rubbed with hot stones will not 'heal' you.
You may like having a seaweed bath or hot stones
the way other women like a bag of chips or a chilled
Mars bar, in which case you pays your money and you
takes your choice. But the bullshit that all women are
stressed-out, wounded and in need of – wait for it
– holistic healing is just that. Bullshit.

- If you get fat, get over it. You have a baby, you get fat. You stay home to mind the kids for a few years, you get fat. You like food, you get fat. You're too busy to count calories, you get fat. Get over it. Don't advertise it by apologies, by wearing cheap thrown-together clothes or by slumping when you walk. It's a fact, like your fingerprints. It doesn't define you unless you let it.

- If he hits you, leave him. Never mind how grief-stricken he is next day. Never mind the circumstances. If you stay, he'll hit you again. If you go, you'll manage.

- Don't manipulate. Some of the best women I've seen on training courses started by trying to manipulate the group by talking about how scared they were or how bad they were at presenting/selling/interviewing. As Oscar Wilde put it: 'There is luxury in self-reproach. When we blame ourselves, we feel no one else has a right to blame us.' Eschew that luxury. It does you no good and it's a pain in the ass for everybody else.

Janis Joplin, rock musician
Don't compromise yourself. You're all you've got.

Máire Geoghegan-Quinn, former Minister for Justice
The best advice I ever got was from my Mum. I was in boarding school in my final year and wanted more than anything to do medicine. She advised me to forget about it – it took six or seven years, I would meet a fellow in the middle of it, fall in love, get married and end up with no qualification to go back to if I ever needed to support myself later on. Instead she advised

me to do primary school teaching – just two years in college. She said that if I really wanted to do medicine I could always go back to college later.

Was her advice right? Looking back now, I believe it was – because what she predicted came true.

Why was she so determined for me to have a career I could go back to (should I decide to take time out to have babies)? She was a teacher herself and resented the fact that when she got married she had no choice but to give up her job because of the marriage ban. She felt strongly that only by choice should a woman be financially dependent on a man.

She was way before her time…

Jilly Cooper, author
Never drink black coffee at lunchtime. It will keep you awake all afternoon.

Mary Wollstonecraft, feminist and author, A Vindication of the Rights of Woman
Women are told from their infancy, and taught by the example of their mothers, that a little knowledge of human weakness, justly termed cunning, softness of temper, outward obedience, and a scrupulous attention to a puerile kind of propriety, will obtain for them the protection of man; and should they be beautiful, everything else is needless, for at least twenty years of their lives. (from)

Mrs Harris, who shot her lover and served a lengthy prison sentence for it
[Dogs] seem to read your moods…the way you once hoped husbands and children would but rarely did. Every woman who lives in a man's world, and we all still do, should have a dog to sort of complete a man's personality. You can even laugh at them and they don't mind.

Maureen Smyth, Director, Forensic Science Laboratory

My 'best advice' line is, I'm afraid, clichéd: 'You're never too old', from my father who is 100 and who, for example, bought a second-hand trailer tent when he was eighty. Note: he is not still using it but is just back from Lourdes with the Meath Pilgrimage so you could say he is still travelling!) Might explain why I still play hockey with some people who, at a small stretch, could be my grandchildren; and if I won the Lottery I would probably go back and study again…for the crack!

Jane Fonda, actor

For thousands of years, boys have been taught that 'real men' are tough and emotionless and respond to every slight, real or imagined, with violence.

Girls have been taught that 'real women' should please men and put up with their violence. This patriarchal paradigm has done terrible harm to both genders, cutting off men from their innate empathy and women from their innate strength. As we continue to reclaim our power, we must help create a new masculinity that is less vulnerable to shaming – a feminist masculinity, if you will. Mothers and grandmothers, teachers, coaches, and mentors, let's help our boys become emotionally literate. Let's teach them it's okay to cry, to forgive, to express love. Maybe they'll set a good example for their fathers.

Adi Roche, Founder, Chernobyl Children's Project International

'Work to your strengths and talents. Don't try and be something you're not. Trust in the process. Be humble always. You don't have to be an "expert" when you trust in your own knowledge and experiences. When you give openly, honestly and with the right motivation the return "profit" will bring you peace and happiness beyond your wildest dreams.' I draw on this a lot, particularly when I feel inadequate and unsure. Said to me in conversation by a friend from New Zealand who is also an activist.

Mae West, actor
Keep a diary. One day it'll keep you.

Phyllis Diller, comedian
Be nice to your children, for they will choose your rest home.

Una Halligan, Government Affairs Director, Hewlett Packard
One February evening when I was doing the dreaded ironing and listening to the RTE1, I heard a discussion about life choices. A speaker made the observation that life was a journey and we are all on our own particular road on this journey. If you are happy with your life and where your road is taking you, then just keep going, but if you don't want to end up as you are, then you need to find the road that leads to a different destination. It won't just happen: you need to see the signs for the crossroads and make that diversion.

At this point in my life I was a full-time mother with two children aged ten and eight and I knew I wanted more from my life. I had toyed with the idea of going back to college and this piece of advice galvanised me into action. Next day I rang UCD and made enquiries and I began a full-time Bachelor of Social Science degree the following October. It was a life-changing experience that led to a dramatically different life journey.

I still hate ironing…

8

Advice to Men

Men get advice all the time. For-your-own-good advice. Delivered by professionals with an accompanying shrug: Men! What can you do with them?

Take health advice. Men don't. In fact, if you listen to the health promotion folk, they'll give you a portrait of your average man with a corporation on him hanging out over his jeans, lungs like Brillo pads from smoking, arteries siltier than the Mississippi delta, blood pressure scary high and cholesterol ditto. But quite content. Quite comfortable that any of these days he'll get back to being as fit as he was when he'd take on any man on the football field. Not worried that anything bad is going to happen to him, in fact, quite certain that predictions of bad things lined up for lads like him are a) dreamed up by journalists who are a bit short of ideas, b) dreamed up by doctors looking for more business, c) dreamed up by their wives because it gives the missus a free pass to nag.

That *laissez faire* approach extends into sexual health: young men in particular, like bad actors, are convinced it'll be all right on the night, even if they've no condom and their prospective partner could be luminous with cross-bred STDs.

The other kind of advice men ignore, not because they disagree with it, but because they don't even notice it, is advice from women on changing the workplace. Ambitious male executives pay attention to their bonuses, their share options, their semi-annual reviews, their promotion prospects and their 360-degree feedback reports, but days devoted to work–life balance or taking your child to work with you tend to take them by surprise and irritate them to a swollen-faced silent fury. The fury is silent because they have 'that crap' filed under 'politically correct', and therefore don't articulate what they feel, which is: 'What a waste of bloody time, what the hell is the point of bringing a four-year-old to work? OK. If some moron has decided we're going to do this bilge, let's get it over with in one day and belt up thereafter with the holistic, family-friendly stuff, please.'

Just as there's a bunch of medical advisers standing by with pumps full of good stuff they want to inject into men, there's always a bunch of women standing by with pumps full of advice for men on how to turn the workplace more female. Since the Industrial Revolution, the workplace has been run by men along male lines and they like it that way and it works for them and for a lot of the women who now work side by side with them, but a banked-up mountain of unaccepted advice to men about the workplace still exists, including suggestions that meetings should be quite different, that the patriarchal structure of businesses needs to be modified, and the profit bottom line abandoned.

Men go glazed when any of this is mentioned. They don't even fight the underlying assumption, which is that women are a lot better, as human beings go, than men are, and that if you let enough of them loose with a free enough hand, the end result will be light, happiness and peace, with nobody in the office ever pissed off at anybody else. This kind of advice men see as a kind of durance test: if they listen and nod for long enough, it'll go away.

Example? Float Jane Fonda's suggestion from the end of the

previous chapter past any busy male work colleague and watch the
eye-glaze spread.

The kind of advice men like, on the other hand, tends to come
from one of two sources: war and sport.

Not exclusively. Mention must be made of literature. Well, no,
that might be pitching it a tad high. Mention must be made of just
one particular book. A great big goddamn doorstopper of a book.
Called *The Fountainhead*, by Ayn Rand. A small but constantly-
renewed sub-group of men has been converted by *The Fountainhead*
since it was first published in the 1940s. Which is amazing, given
that it's all about architecture, by a writer who wasn't an architect.

Ayn Rand was mostly a self-created entity. Born in Russia to
wealthy parents, she took a dim view of communism when her
family's business was taken from them, and got to the US as quickly
as she could thereafter. *The Fountainhead* is about an architect named
Roark who is True To Himself. Will he build the pretty buildings
people want? No, by God, he won't. He will build what he wants to
build and people will flock to his door. They flock enough for the
reader who perseveres to the end of the book to get the message
that the individual is what matters. Never mind that the rest of
the world regards naked self-interest as having a few drawbacks,
in social terms. Individualism is where it's at. You grow your own
standards, you identify your own target, you build your own tank
to get there, and if any of what Leona Helmsley called the 'little
people who pay taxes' get a bit pulverised along the way, they had
it coming.

For some reason, this overstated arrogance-as-ideology appeals
to some men. (It may also appeal to some women. I just haven't
found one yet.) They go on *Fountainhead* courses to be taught how
to be more individual than they already are. The good thing is that
Fountainhead guys seem to be the business equivalent of mules:

they don't breed. So the percentage of men influenced by Ayn Rand stays mercifully minuscule.

For the majority of men, advice coming from sport or war tends to have a certain resonance. Sport because they buy into the school team and practise for hours in the hope of getting further; and because sport is like MRSA: it's all around us, but infects only those already weakened. Sport influences men already weakened by family traditions and childhood hopes. When you come from a clan where every man older than you can name who fumbled the penalty in 1933, then the chances are that when someone quotes a question like 'Where's your effing spirit?' everybody in the house can call out the name of the person who said it and when.

That kind of lineage leads to men drawing life lessons from sporting successes or disasters. The kind of man who might – if he wasn't glued to Setanta Sports on the box – read *The Fountainhead* is the kind of man who believes you have to be like Roy Keane in Saipan. Cut to the chase. Tell it like it is. Stand up for what you believe in. Stomp on those who don't believe in the same sporting verities.

Sporting advice, extrapolated to apply to every other challenge, really starts with Keep At It. Hence the famous story about golfer Joe Carr being congratulated on a major victory by someone who told him he was very lucky.

'That's true,' the genial Carr replied. 'And the more I practise, the luckier I get.'

Next bit of guidance is Never Give Up. The moral lesson here is that no physical handicap can get in your way if you muster up sufficient determination. This is supported by evidence of visually impaired people climbing Everest and athletes who have had their legs amputated running marathons on prostheses.

After that comes Be a Good Team Member. No solo runs in

team games. Fit in. Champion others, not yourself. Be like a marine: subordinate your individuality, right down to your personal survival instinct, to the needs of your colleagues. Semper Fi. (Clearly the team member types do not belong to the *Fountainhead* cult.)

Just how any of this applies to running a call centre or setting up a restaurant beats me, but men seem to like it.

They also get turned on by references to battle. It's men who buy books about the insights to be drawn from Attilla the Hun, Sun Tsu or General Patton. Curiously, nobody has to my knowledge produced a book of management advice drawn from the philosophies of the outstandingly successful commander of WWII: Dwight D. Eisenhower. This could be because Ike wasn't much for general statements. He just did things. Like win the war. Or it could be because he took such a commonsense understated approach to leadership, even when it took the form of the presidency of one of the great powers, requiring his administrators to condense the most complex issues into one page for him to read and decide upon, because there was golf to be played.

Generally, though, when men seek out and quote military leaders, they tend to be the showy ones.

The one thing men could do with a little helpful advice on is apologising. They don't like doing it and they're rotten at it when there's no alternative. P.G. Wodehouse summed up the male attitude when he said: 'It's a good rule in life never to apologise. The right sort of people do not want apologies, and the wrong sort take a mean advantage of them.'

The curious thing is that women have no problem apologising. Even when they haven't done the fell deed, they'll apologise to get it the hell over with and move on to the next issue. But then, if, as a gender, you've been brought up to think in terms of guarding open goals, holding the line, defending the pass, repelling the invader

and taking the next hill, saying 'Sorry' is going to make you feel
like a big girl's blouse. To avoid it, men have developed a series of
apology impersonators. They look like an apology, they squeak like
an apology, but they're sure as hell not a real apology.

Here's an example. Let's imagine you – a male – come to stay
in my house for a week and, on one evening when I fail to provide
dinner for you, you barbeque my budgie. You're now seeking
forgiveness for this.

The first kind of apology to avoid is the *conditional apology*.
That's the one where you say, 'I apologise if you feel upset about your
budgie loss.' That takes no responsibility for doing in the bird, but
instead sends the message that if I wasn't such a wimp, I wouldn't
be making such a song and dance about it. In addition, it seeks to
objectify the issue. Instead of you killing my budgie, which is up
close, personal and takes ownership of the crime, the avian demise
becomes an external happening, owned by nobody in particular.

The *dead speak* apology is where you tell me you feel sure the
budgie would have wanted to sacrifice iself to take away your hunger
pangs. (This one is mostly used by celebs shacking up with indecent
haste after a bereavement: 'It's OK, my dead partner would've
wanted me to "move on with my life."')

The *could have been worse* apology is where you grovel for
murdering my budgie, but draw my attention to the fact that my
goldfish are still circling their bowl whereas you could've had them
on toast for an appetiser.

The *legal advice* apology is the one you come up with if you
have legal training. It says that hurt may been experienced (no
specifics as to who's hurting or certainty as to the hurt itself) as
the possible result of a budgie issue (no ownership of anti-budgie
action) so, without prejudice, (no admission of guilt implied) regret
is expressed (by nobody in particular).

The *minimise the offence* is the worst of all forms of bad apology. It effectively says it wasn't much of a budgie to start with. So get over it. And anyway, look at all you could do with the feathers…

If I could give one gender-specific piece of advice to men, it would be in how to apologise. A great apology is fast, unsought, unconditional, indicates the gravity of the offence and the level of misery caused, and gets around to a suggested methodology for kissing it better. Professor Daniel Dennett, Director of the Center for Cognitive Studies at Tufts University, says that the natural human reaction to a mistake is embarrassment and anger, and you have to work hard to overcome these emotional reactions.

'Try to acquire the weird practice of savouring your mistakes, delighting in uncovering the strange quirks that led you astray,' advises Professor Dennet. 'Then, once you have sucked out all the goodness to be gained from having made them, you can cheerfully forget them, and go on to the next big opportunity.'

Gay Byrne, broadcaster

The best advice I ever got was: 'Prepare yourself and the opportunity will come.' That advice was given to me way way early on, by a man whose name I can't even remember. He was in amateur dramatics – ran a little outfit in Westland Row called the National Art Theatre, which I joined when I was sixteen or seventeen.

'You have a splendid voice,' he told me – and he was the first to say so. 'With that instrument,' he went on, 'you can go anywhere.'

He was dead right. I have believed throughout my life that if you prepare and keep preparing, you get somewhere, somehow, *because* you have prepared, and probably also because you are sufficiently above the norm, when you get the opportunity, you take the ball and run with it. If you are not prepared, if you do not have that belief that the opportunity will present itself, opportunity, when it arrives, will slip away.

If any of the readers of this book remembers Eamonn Andrews, he was my hero. He prepared himself in every way he could, from his teens. He did amateur dramatics, joined a debating society, did every crap sports commentary he could – all of that. When he first went to London, Stuart McPherson, a Canadian guy, was king in the BBC as far as sport was concerned. He was Jimmy Magee and everybody else rolled into one. He ruled the roost. Then his da died in Toronto, where he had been running a newspaper combine.

'I'm going back to take over the business,' McPherson announced, and off he went to take up the reins. Suddenly, the BBC had a problem.

'There's a young fella here called Eamonn Andrews,' someone said. 'Let's give him a go.'

Which they did. And Eamonn, because he had done all of the years of preparation, was able to grab the ball and run with it. He had spent all his time getting ready for this amazingly unusual opportunity, an opportunity nobody could have predicted, and so he could step into McPherson's shoes and deliver.

I've always taken a leaf out of that book and passed that on to various people down the years…

Delta Burke, actor
If you want to say it with flowers, a single rose says, 'I'm cheap.'

Miss Piggy
Only time will heal your broken heart, just as only time will heal his broken arms and legs.

General Patton
If a man does his best, what else is there?

Keith Nolan, photographer and restaurateur

Throughout my life, faced with platitudes, quotes, well-meaning meanderings, – 'look deep into yourself' or 'ask God'-type nonsense – I nodded sagely, pretended to listen and then did what I wanted to do or had intended to do. I never got any advice other than what other people wanted me to act on, i.e., bank managers advising on insurance policies, parents on careers and my son telling me to stop embarrassing him. Beware all experts and people who think they know best…

Padhraic Ó Ciardha, leasphríomhcheannasaí, TG4

As a young broadcast journalist, I found myself complaining to a colleague about having been assigned a few very prickly and uncooperative technicians. It had seemed to me that these (men) seemed more intent on intimidating me or at least not acceding to requests to do things a certain way than on doing a good job together.

My more experienced, wiser colleague said, 'The thing to do there is to wait until the guy is about to do one of his tricks on the machinery some day and then say, "I'd love some day if you had time to show me why you do it that way." You'll be surprised.'

I did as I was bid and, as predicted, my ogres turned into charming and helpful colleagues, happy and eager to show a neophyte some of the tricks of their trade. It was as if a grandad had been waiting for years for the chance to show his grandchild how to cast a fly or swing a hurley.

Some day I hope someone will ask me!

9

ADVICE ON WORK AND CAREERS

Perhaps because we spend so much of our lives at work, that's the area that generates most advice, sought and unsought. Business books, offering the ten rules on anything, sell. Interviews with successful business leaders appear in magazines and newspapers. Billions are spent every year, by companies and individuals, on consultants.

And out of all of that, here's the reality: when advice is general, it has little effect, but lasts forever. When advice is individual and based on positive observation of one human being's potential, it lasts with that person, but may never escape to the wider world.

Take, for example, *Proverbs* 12:24. 'Work hard and be a leader; be lazy and become a slave,' it advises.

Although most managers don't quote the Bible when they give that advice, it gets delivered every day in some organisation somewhere. As does the advice of Willy Loman, the eponymous character in Arthur Miller's play *Death of a Salesman*: 'The man who makes an appearance in the business world, the man who creates personal interest, is the man who gets ahead. Be liked and you will never want.'

In that statement lies a grain of truth. Not a big enough grain to save poor Willie, or to get promotion for a lot of really pleasant people in the workplace. It does, however, tend to make life easier for the other people around the man or woman whose career has tanked, and it may even make their own life happier. Being miserable when you're not appreciated has no payoff. The definitive example is the Japanese Schindler, a spy in Lithuania during WWII named Chiune Sugihara.

Although his official title was consul-general, Sugihara's main job was to uncover German and Russian military secrets and feed them back to his government. If they got transit visas from the Japanese consulate, Lithuanian Jews could get through the Soviet Union to Curaçao. He wrote some. Then, in 1940, he met a delegation that indicated that 'some' was not enough, because Jews were being transported to concentration camps and exterminated in their millions.

He cabled his government seeking permission. Permission refused. He cabled again. The previous response was reiterated. He cabled a third time. No change. He issued the visas anyway. He wrote them by hand, completing three hundred every day. At night, his wife massaged his aching arm. In all, he wrote 3,500 visas. Since an entire family could travel on one visa, the precise numbers of Jews he saved has never been established.

'I have to do something,' he told his wife. 'A young man comes to my home for protection. Is he dangerous? No. Is he a spy? No. Is he a traitor? No. He's just a Jewish teenager who wants to live. I may have to disobey my government, but if I don't, I will be disobeying God.'

After the war, Sugihara went back to Japan, where he was dismissed from his government job because of his wartime actions and found it difficult to get employment elsewhere. He took odd jobs to get by, was miserable, and made no secret of his misery, always appearing to be 'dour and depressed'. One man who worked with him said he was 'a difficult man to approach. He felt himself above others but had lost face.' Sugihara – who died in 1986, his heroism still unrecognised – is the definitive example of a man whose real situation cannot be reached by that facile perennial advice to the disappointed, disaffected and disenfranchised: 'Get over it.'

One former diplomat who managed to transcend career catastrophe was a Florentine in the fifteenth century, who, at twenty-nine, became Head of the Second Chancery in the Florentine Republic, with the task of managing foreign affairs. For fourteen years, Niccolo Machiavelli went off to Germany and France on diplomatic missions, reporting back to his bosses with a detailed clarity that had a heavy influence on policy-making.

In 1512, as a result of wars between several European States, his boss, the ruler, fled for his life and his successor, Cardinal Giulio de' Medici, removed Machiavelli from office and exiled him to his small farm. He was shamed. Powerless. Impoverished. As if all that wasn't bad enough, his name turned up in a document about possible conspiracies against the Medicis, so he was arrested, imprisoned and tortured.

When he got back to his farm and his family, Machiavelli began to write. What he wrote was a manual on politics and war. He seems to have hoped it would ingratiate him with the Medicis, who would slap their foreheads and say 'Mamma Mia, how did we ever think we could survive or succeed without the constant advice of this big brain?' That never happened. The most Machiavelli may have got, during his lifetime, out of the exercise of writing *The Prince*, was the vicarious pleasure of advising his mythical patron.

Post mortem, however, his book has had enormous popularity. It's always in print in different translations and with commentaries by different contemporary scholars. People who haven't read his works regard him as synonymous with evil, duplicity and venom. The reason his advice turns up in business courses, however, is that so much of it is commonsensical, and applies to a new manager just as readily as it would have applied to a medieval prince.

For example, he advises a new ruler to dish out all the bad news in one humungous serving at the beginning of his reign. Niccolo matched this by advising the new ruler, by contrast, to dole out rewards, promotions and praise over a protracted period of time, keeping the potentially disloyal on side in the hope of preferment while building up a body of committed supporters. Makes sense.

Machiavelli's advice is a lot wiser, in psychological terms, than some of what is currently passing as helpful to managers, like telling them to categorise colleagues into blue- or yellow-hat people according to their characteristics. The Florentine under-stood that every system develops its own pecking order and that within pecking orders, some behaviours are predictable and should be anticipated and coped with by a leader. Since he lived in a period of unceasing war, his approach is necessarily combative. It is, nonetheless, instructive, whether you're in business or in politics or – perhaps most of all – if you operate within a voluntary group. Charities and voluntary groups have a warm and cuddly image. Many of them, nonetheless, make Machiavelli's war-torn Europe look like a doddle to run.

One of Machiavelli's big fans was Lord McAlpine, the former treasurer of the Conservative party. He thought the Florentine's realism about human nature and behaviour was spot-on, whereas he thought Alexander the Great, the much-admired military strategist from the fourth century BC, was a bit obvious, with advice like: 'Speed is the essence of war. Take advantage of the enemy's unpreparedness. Travel by unexpected routes. Strike him where he has taken no precautions.' That's *so* helpful if you're trying to sell a new piece of software you've developed.

Much better advice can be drawn from the behaviour of the

German Kaiser before the First World War. He knew he was about to embark on a sustained campaign unprecedented in war-making, which would require resources, supply lines and systems of which none of his military had any experience. Operating on the principle that you should always copy the best in the business, he asked for advice from Ringling Brothers Circus. They refused to help him. So he sent spies to get jobs with the circus. Those spies were able to observe the level of advance planning required to ensure that fodder for elephants, lions and horses was present at the next stop before the circus pulled down the tent in the location where it was currently playing – and the circus methods were faithfully applied to the German army.

Dell, the computer company, copied Alexander the Great, who died in 323 BC, having established himself as a genius at moving large numbers of well-fed troops speedily to the point where they would be most effective.

The latest trend in the US is to see Jesus as the ultimate advice-giver in business terms. I can't see it catching on in Ireland, given our current preoccupation with not favouring any one religion over another, but it does have its points.

'Cast your bread on the waters and it will return to you after many days,' is not bad advice for an investor.

'Turn the other cheek,' can work in office politics, just as it could work in Roman times.

Whether it comes from religion or an historic general, the best advice is to regard a setback as a necessary stage on the road to success. Especially if you're a writer. For example, the guys who wrote *Chicken Soup for the Soul* got rejection notices from thirty-three publishers. These rejections fulfilled their agent's prediction that 'a book of soppy stories would never sell.' The two writers fired their agent and set themselves up at a book fair, where 134 further publishers rejected their 'book of soppy stories'. They eventually decided to publish it themselves. They have now sold well in excess of 100 million copies of that original book and its follow-ups, and all the titles are still selling.

e.e.cummings did much the same. Fed up with rejections, he borrowed money from his mother and printed his book himself. This gave him the opportunity to list all the publishers who had turned him down. He laid the names out on the page in the shape of a funeral urn.

One of the reasons the *Chicken Soup* authors succeeded is that they took advice from Dr M. Scott Peck, author of another bestseller that won't go away: *The Road Less Travelled.*

'Let me tell you boys you can make $40 million in twelve years, but you got to do it yourselves,' he told them. 'You have to do just one thing. You have to do a media appearance every day for the rest of your life. You can tape twenty in one day and be done for the month.'

The advice to get a high profile for yourself or your product is more likely to be given now than at any time in the past. Although, back in 1843, an article in the *Edinburgh Review* said that:

> The grand principle of modern existence is notoriety; we live and move and have our being in print. What Curran said of Byron, that 'he wept for the press and wiped his eyes with the public,' may now be predicated of everyone who is striving for any sort of distinction. He must not only work, but eat, drink, walk, talk, hunt, shoot, give parties and travel in the newspapers. The universal inference is that if a man be not known he cannot be worth knowing. In this state of things it is useless to swim against the stream, and folly to differ

from our contemporaries; a prudent youth will purchase the last edition of *The Art of Rising in the World*, or *Every Man His Own Fortune-Maker*, and sedulously practice the main precept it enjoys – never to omit an opportunity of placing your name in printed characters before the world. We live and move and have our being in print.

The *Edinburgh Review* writer, a century and a half back, nailed the Paris Hilton/Nicole Richie/Britney Spears syndrome, whereby people of modest talent and achievement become more famous than world leaders. The syndrome makes nonsense of all the advice every kid gets in school about working hard, telling the truth, eating properly and staying away from drugs.

Each of the three got plenty of advice. From judges. From doctors. From record producers. From family. From media commentators. Their reaction was a version of Teresa Heinz Kerry's famous response to an intrusive journalist during her husband's presidential campaign: 'Why don't you just shove it?' You can understand why. If behaving badly gets you more coverage and more offers than behaving 'properly', then critical advice must seem *so* last century. Or even so three centuries ago. Because there's always been a niche for the pretty but worthless. It used to be called royalty. Marie Antoinette's behaviour was eerily similar to that of Princess Diana. And all the good advice in the world wouldn't have shifted either of them off their path of self-destruction.

Any ambitious person in business should read extensively, and with a massive pinch of salt metaphorically present at all times. Because much of the advice coming from the hugely successful managers or entrepreneurs is post-factum rationalisation of sheer bloody luck. Nobody who makes billions and creates a global business wants to believe that they just happened to be in the right place at the right time, so they write a story for themselves which attributes the success to their courage, insight, capacity to lead or physical fitness. That story creates a myth of invincibility. Hence, Sam Walton, who was lucky enough to start a business when people had cars and were beginning to run out of time, so they wanted to buy everything in one place cheaply, created Wal Mart. Bully for him. The myth of the Wal Mart approach and systems developed fast, once he had written his account of his life and died. That myth was shown to have a number of large holes in it when Wal Mart moved into some major European markets and fell on its nose in them.

Business leadership, like military leadership, cannot be learned by absorbing and applying 'The Ten Rules of Management' or 'The Seven Secrets of Leading People'. Business leaders cannot be built like an adobe hut, using dollops of mud (meaning advice) from the careers of other leaders, present or past. Great leaders are as different from one another as the rest of us are different from one another. The advice one of them gives will be discountenanced by the behaviour of another. Ben Franklin, for example, arguably the biggest pain-in-the-ass advice giver since Aesop, came up with the tip that goes 'Early to bed, early to rise, makes a man healthy, wealthy and wise.'

Tell that to Churchill, who not only didn't get up much before lunchtime, but napped during the day and didn't go to bed early.

The one bit of advice to be drawn from the lives of most, although not all, business and war success figures, is that communication is crucial. The most successful generals or managers are the ones who listen, who can create an atmosphere where subordinates are not afraid to tell the truth and bring the bad news and who, having gathered in all the data, can make a decision and have the skill to communicate that decision throughout their organisation or army with sufficient clarity and passion to motivate the troops to implement it.

John Banville, author and Booker prizewinner

I'm afraid I didn't have a wise old granny or the like to give me advice, and if I had, and she had, I most likely wouldn't have taken it. I'm tempted to echo – who was it? – whose father strongly advised him when he was young above all to avoid folk dancing and incest...

But I do remember first reading, many years ago, Rilke's 'Duino Elegies' and being struck by this passage, which I've never forgotten, and which seems the best possible advice a writer could take:

> Praise this world to the Angel, not the untellable: you can't impress him with the splendour you've felt; in the cosmos where he more feelingly feels you're only a novice. So show him some simple thing, refashioned by age after age, till it lives in our hands and eyes as a part of ourselves. Tell him things. (Translation by J. B. Leishman and Stephen Spender.)

Hilary Humphreys, Professor of Clinical Microbiology

One piece of advice that immediately comes to mind came from my late father, a shrewd and wise man, even if I may say so myself. When presented with a report or story of what somebody did, when it appeared as if the action of the individual was utterly indefensible, his initial reaction would be to be dubious at accepting the story at face value. He would state 'There are at least two sides to every story.' How right I have found that advice to be, over the years.

Jean Callanan, marketing consultant
The best advice I ever got was by example rather than words.

I was a brand manager in my mid-twenties working for Guinness (now Diageo of course) and I made a poor judgement call in relation to promotion. The result was not just bad press publicity but the entire salesforce had to drop selling and normal business and go and withdraw the visibility material from the 10,000-plus pubs in the country.

I had seriously screwed up! Having confessed and put in place all the actions needed to reduce the impact of my mistake I withdrew to my office guilty and totally lacking in self-confidence. I sat there after the others went home, feeling miserable.

All of a sudden, around seven o'clock, the then sales director, Pat Healy, arrived in my office with a bottle of gin in one pocket, and tonic and two glasses in the other. He smiled and said, 'I thought you might need some support.' We sat for half an hour, drinking and chatting about life in general.

I was several rungs down the hierarchy from a director, and it was the marketing director who was my boss, yet this man whose life I had made very difficult that day had crossed Thomas Street from his office to a building he rarely visited and climbed two floors in a fairly deserted office block to give me some support.

He showed me true leadership that day. I remember some years later in a Unilever office in Hamburg bringing coffee, cake and words of encouragement late in the evening to a junior manager who had made a poor call on an issue that could have cost the company millions, and was sitting there miserable. She wasn't my direct report or responsibility, but I remembered the excellent example shown in James's Gate all those years before.

Mother Teresa
Let no one ever come to you without leaving better and happier.

Ursula Halligan, TV3

Whenever I am overwhelmed with rage at the behaviour of another or at some perceived injustice which leaves me teetering on the brink of banging out a resignation letter; sending off a snotty text or venting my anger in a phone call – I've learned to pause and recall the advice of a dear friend who once counselled me to 'Sleep on it first.'

It's one of the best pieces of advice I've ever received. A good night's sleep can change your perspective, clarify your objectives and allow you work out a more pragmatic and realistic way of dealing with the problem in a way that acting impulsively or in anger rarely can.

Jerry West, NBA [National Basketball Association] star

You can't get too much done in life if you only work on the days when you feel good.

Stanley Marcus, Chairman Emeritus, Nieman Marcus

You achieve customer satisfaction when you sell merchandise that doesn't come back to a customer who does.

Alan Crosbie, CEO, Thomas Crosbie Holdings

Around the time I became CEO of the Examiner Group, a very good friend who is also a management consultant gave me a piece of advice that was key to what I achieved.

'Don't do anything for six months,' he said. 'But if you haven't done a whole load by eighteen months, resign.'

Salvador Dali

Have no fear of perfection. You will never achieve it.

Woody Allen, film director

80 per cent of success is showing up.

Gerry Mullins, author of Ireland's Number#1 Nazi

When I was a cub scout in Mount Melleray aged nine I bought an interesting little card in the monastery shop from one of the monks that said: 'When you come to die, make sure the only thing you have left to do is die.' That had an interesting effect and I've tried to abide by it.

When I was in my late twenties and was clearly having an unhappy time in the financial services industry, I took advice from several people. Referring to me taking jobs I didn't like but because I liked the money, one person told me the definition of madness was trying the same thing each time but expecting different results.

Another said: 'You will never succeed in a job you don't like.' Taking both on board I switched to journalism and it has worked.

In recent times I was turned down for a job that I wanted. A friend told me not to be emotional: 'Do not go with your instincts and call them every name under the sun. Do not give it to them right between the eyeballs. The only way for you to make them sorry for not giving you the job is to prove to them that you are so good that they must have made a mistake.' This advice is difficult to follow and may take a long time before we can know if it is the correct path of not.

Brody Sweeney, Chairman, O'Brien's Sandwich Bars

Don't worry about how much you think the other guy is making – concentrate on your own game.

I was very prone to spending my day being stressed about how well my competitors were doing and how much money they were making and wondering about how they could be doing it, instead of putting all that wasted energy into my own business.

Mary Finan, Chairman, RTE

I've got great advice from parents and friends over the years which I've put to good use, including two pieces from Tom Savage: He suggests you should ask, 'Is that your final offer?' when you are being offered a job and you don't want to enter into a Dutch auction. It concentrates the mind and works!

His other fantastic tip was to follow a moving/emotional part of a speech with a joke or amusing anecdote – it clears the air and allows people to laugh. I used it in my WHPR [Wilson Hartnell Public Relations] goodbye speech and it worked a dream. I was terrified I would cry and I didn't.

Others:

1. Honesty is invincible.
2. Manage your life (only you can).
3. Never make assumptions – they're usually wrong!
4. Never put in writing something you would not wish to see on the front page of your morning newspaper.
5. Always do your best – then you will not have regrets that you should have put more thought /time into something (from my father).
6. You need to be disciplined to have the freedom to do what you want. For example, if you want to run at 6am, you must be in bed by 10pm – mundane example but it works across the spectrum of our lives.

Des Lamont, L&P Trust Managers

The best advice I ever got was, 'Opportunity comes to pass, not to pause.' Michael Smurfit said it to me and a colleague in about 1982. It related specifically to the first flurry of interest in Irish Oil shares, but I have used it ever since.

Suzanne Strempek Shea, author and assistant in an American book shop

When I first began at the [book] store, I got into the habit of handing over change with the wish 'Enjoy your *Newsweek*!' Or 'Enjoy your *Fix-it-and-Forget-it-Cookbook*.'

But it's still just my first day on the job at Edwards, and a woman comes in to pick up the two books she'd ordered: Two, count 'em two copies of *The Dual Disorders Recovery Book*...There is the springboard for a host of 'Hey, covering all the bases' type of comments, but Pat, the owner, simply says, 'Here you are,' without adding, as I might be tempted to, 'One for each of you!'

'You gotta love that she wanted two copies,' I say. Pat smiles. I continue poking. 'You must see all types.'

'You do.'

She doesn't say anything else. Then she does: 'As much as you'd like to say something at times, you don't,' she tells me. 'I learned a long time ago not to comment on what people are buying...If they're buying a travel book, I'll say, "Have a nice trip." But if it's something on divorce, a kind of book like that, I don't say anything.'

Linda Cullen. Head of Television, CoCo Television

A great piece of advice I got was from Bunny Carr. I remember him saying, 'When you don't know a thing, just say you don't know it. Don't waste their time or yours no matter how accommodating you think you're being, by trying to find an answer you don't have.' If I don't know something that's exactly what I do – to this day.

My mother always advised me that I could do whatever I want in life and I believed it – though I'm not sure that is advice as much as blind faith...

Mike Nichols, film director

[At the beginning of directing a film with Richard Burton and Elizabeth Taylor.]

It was not only my first day on the picture, it was my first day on a movie set. I had thought and thought about it and had drawn little pictures and made little plans, and Richard and Elizabeth were all made up and ready to go and there were a hundred and fifty men standing around with their arms folded, and I suddenly thought, How do I get them through the door? If the camera is facing the door, won't the door hit the camera when it opens? And if it's far enough, won't they walk into the camera when they come in? I didn't know where to put the camera because I wanted to see them close. And then I thought, If it's too close, the door will hit it. Well, everybody had all sorts of suggestions.

I mean, it was clear that I was in naked panic. And I had special advisers. And finally the cameraman said, 'See, we'll do this and they'll come in and we'll move and we'll pan them and they'll disappear momentarily behind the wall as they walk toward the kitchen and we'll see them reappear again and it will be very interesting.' And I said, 'Well, what's it for?' He said, 'Well, it's interesting.' And I thought, Oh, Christ. Now I have to do this very hard thing. They know more than I do, but I have to decide what it's going to be because I know what I am going to tell and they don't. That was a terrible minute. And I just said, All right. Pull yourself together and do it. And I did. And then, you begin to learn it. You begin to discover what it is. There are various sorts of mysteries that are cleared up by accident...

Actor/singer, Irish – chooses to be anonymous
My mother always said what's for you won't pass you. Means you don't get hung up about things. If they're to be they'll happen. And what's not to be is not to be for a reason.

Doesn't mean you don't put the work into something... just that you don't slit your wrists if it fails. And you can sit back a bit more and let life come to you too.

Other thing was to always be true to yourself. And to understand that everyone has their own reasons for doing something. Mightn't make sense to the rest of us but to try to see it from their perspective. Probably nothing there that you wouldn't get from a thousand other mothers but for what it's worth....

Alice Leahy, Trust Ireland

The best advice I would give anyone is not to be afraid to reject it and do what you feel you have to do. Personally the best decision I ever made was against the 'best' advice I received, and I have always been very sceptical about 'good' advice since.

I still remember vividly the morning I stood in my crisp white uniform surrounded by the monitors and defibrillators, with phones ringing constantly, in Ireland's first intensive care unit of its type which I managed and had been responsible for setting up for the Board of The Royal City of Dublin Hospital, Baggot Street. The expression on the face of the consultant in charge, when I informed him I was leaving my permanent and pensionable job to work with people who were homeless, is still etched in my consciousness. He looked at me solemnly in stunned silence for a few moments before telling me I needed to see a psychiatrist if I was serious about giving up my job for what he saw as a haphazard existence that probably would barely allow me to put bread on the table. Indeed, thinking back his reaction almost suggested I had informed him I intended to become homeless myself!

But that was in the 1970s, when what were seen as good jobs in Ireland were very hard to come by. This did not soften the blow, however, of his suggestion that I needed psychiatric care, assuring me he could open doors to ensure I was seen immediately and would receive the best help available. If anything I felt insulted and more determined to follow my own path so maybe he inadvertently did me a favour.

However, what is even more remarkable, thinking back, is that the level of frustration and disillusionment that apparently abounds in the health service today was also prevalent then. In the early 1970s times were very difficult in healthcare with a real shortage of nurses and agency personnel, if available, filling the gap. Nurses also marched then for better pay and conditions. So what has changed?

Today I feel really privileged to work in a world that is challenging, inspiring and life-enhancing and feel well rewarded for following my own instincts against the so-called best advice available.

Mark Twain, to a would-be author

Agassiz does recommend authors to eat fish, because the phosphorus in it makes brain. So far you are correct. But I cannot help you to a decision about the amount you need to eat – at least not with certainty. If the specimen composition you send is about your fair usual average, I suggest that perhaps a couple of whales would be all you would want for the present. Not the largest kind, but simply good middling-sized whales.

Norman Newcombe, marketing expert

In your working life you should aim to have fun and to earn reasonable money. Periodically you will find that you are not having much fun but he money is great. At other times you find that the fun is mighty but the money is terrible. But if you are having no fun and the money is bad then it's time to change jobs!

Robert Ballagh, artist

In the 1970s, I had had an exhibition in Dublin which had done reasonably well, I suppose. Those were the days, remember, when you couldn't give art away.

I'd gone to New York to see if I could interest an American gallery in my work, and after a lot of hassle, a gallery in Madison Avenue agreed to give me an exhibition. The gallery owner even came to see me in my studio in Dublin. But then complications arose and it was clear it wasn't going to happen.

This meant I had this exhibition which I couldn't put on again in Dublin because I had just had one. I mentioned this to the artist Cecil King and he asked me to come and see him. He sat me down and listened to the story.

'I've a suggestion for you,' he said. 'I suggest you go to the art fair in Basel in Switzerland and see if you can get someone interested in your work there.'

I'd never heard of the Basel Art Fair. I'm not sure I'd even heard of Basel, at that point. My wife and myself had a meeting, decided to draw out the last £150 we had in bank, and bought a return ticket. I pre-booked a B&B for a week and bought a season ticket for the art fair. Very little was left from the £150 at that point.

The only way I can describe the art fair is that it's the [RDS] Spring Show, except, instead of tractors, it's filled with galleries and gallery owners. It's all about the business of selling art. I would arrive up in front of a gallery owner, tell them I was an artist from Ireland and ask if they'd like to look at some slides. No, they wouldn't.

That was Monday. That was Tuesday. That was Wednesday. I was in total despair. I couldn't go out and drown my sorrows, because I didn't have any money. I would have gone home straight away, except the flight ticket was one of those that requires you to stay until Saturday.

Believe it or not, on the Thursday, I went to this Parisian gallery and trotted out the rigmarole to the guy. 'I'll talk to you in a minute,' he said, taking a phone call and gesturing me to a seat.

The minute became two minutes. Then five. Then ten. Fifteen. Twenty.

'OK, let's look at your work,' he eventually said, putting down the phone. He looked very quickly, making two piles out of the slides. 'I'd be very interested in those,' he said, pointing at one pile. 'How much?'

Because I was totally naïve, I hadn't thought out the answer to that question. Off the top of my head I quoted a price.

'If I take them, I get them at 50 per cent discount,' was his response.

'Ooooh.'

'You want to have time to think about it, come back in half an hour.'

I didn't even have the money to phone home. So I went back to him.

'OK,' I said, 'but I can't afford to transport them over here.'

No problem, he said, he'd take care of having them crated up and freighted to Paris. The amount I agreed to was something like £3,000, which, in the 1970s, was a lot of money for an artist. Feeling a lot better, I decided to press ahead and approach other owners, and perhaps because of my slightly more confident air, a gallery in London invited me to show there, and then a Swiss gallery offered me thirteen shows in Europe in the next couple of years.

Cecil King's advice gave me a huge breakthrough and I was always grateful for it.

John Lonergan, Governor, Mountjoy Prison

Mercy is so important. I'm beginning to doubt that there's much mercy in modern Ireland. Everything is about rights and justice. But mercy is more important than justice.

I was lucky that early on, I had a great old tutor and mentor as a governor years and years ago. He's dead now, God be good to him, and his name was Paddy Kelly. Amazing man. The humanity of him. I never saw anybody with such humanity – a humanity that would be regarded as weakness nowadays in the modern world and within modern management.

The thing that used to really worry him more than anything was when he had to make a decision about someone else's life in terms of transferring them or punishing them or whatever. The level of anxiety he used to show beforehand and then he'd reflect afterwards to be sure he'd done the right thing.

The kindest thing I saw, when he came to Limerick in 1969, was he went around and talked to the prisoners.

'What's the food like?' he asked them.

'Shit,' they said.

'That's the first thing we're going to do," he said. 'Improve the food – because that is what actually connects everybody: food. A good breakfast and a good dinner and nice food means you're communicating to people: *You're a person, you're important.*'

It's simple, but when you think about it, four times a day, a prisoner will eat. It makes such sense, as opposed to the theories from psychology books. It's human stuff. Basic stuff. He listened, too, and listening is so important.

I've met more bastards in power and in bureaucracy than I ever met in prison. But the few that shone out all the time were people who had humanity and concern, who saw that people in prison are at a low point in terms of status. Encouragement, positivity, kindness, all the things that connect with people can make an amazing impact on people who are probably never treated like that. You have to remember that prison is the only place where a lot of those people have rights. *Prison* is the only place they have rights.

The other bit of advice was from my mother. About honesty. She was mad for honesty in terms that sound stupid now. If I came home from the shop with the wrong change in my favour, she'd make me go back with it.

That honesty, and a huge generosity she had, never left us and we thought it was second nature. But it wasn't second nature. It was *our* nature because she ingrained it into us.

Lieutenant General Dermot Earley, Defence Forces Chief of Staff
The Dean of St Nathy's College, Ballaghaderreen, County Roscommon, spoke to our class one morning when I was a student there in the early 1960s. Fr James Gavigan (RIP) was addressing us after a prefect had gone a bit overboard in administering corporal punishment as a result of a misdemeanour by student.

Fr Gavigan demanded that we, the students, obey the rules of the college, and said that our behaviour must be of the highest standard at all times. He also spoke of the responsibilities of prefects and of what was expected of those in charge. During this part of his address he stated the following, which has never left me: 'If you want to know what a person is really like, give him a bit of authority.'

I don't know what my thoughts were about that statement on that morning in the classroom in St Nathy's but I do recall that the importance of being fair in your dealings with others when in authority was the impression I took away.

As I progressed through military life that piece of advice was most helpful in my development as a leader. It was not just how I acted myself, but being able to assess the make-up of those in authority: how they used it or abused it and how they could become better leaders. In those early days in the army, I also learned to be "fair, firm and friendly'. My experience has been that people will do anything for you provided they perceive they are being treated fairly. That fairness is solidified by a word of praise and thanks from the leader. What you are really doing is winning the support and respect of those whom you lead.

In my reading over the years, I have never found the source of Fr Gavigan's piece of advice, but recently, when listening to a young officer speak on developing young leaders, I heard her state at one point, 'If you want to know what a person is really like, give him or her a bit of authority.' When questioned, she wasn't sure where this advice had come from, but said, 'It is good advice.' I agreed, quietly recalling that morning in St Nathy's. For, in dealing with people, it was the best advice I ever got...

10

ADVICE ON POLITICS

I am on first name terms with a dozen Gardai I've never met. I telephone them. I don't mean to telephone them, but I dial the number and they pick up.

'Hello.' Now, mark that – Hello with a full stop. Not a comma to encourage a developing relationship. Not a question mark to indicate interest in the caller. Just a greeting.

That greeting is the non-mating call of the garda driver who's got stuck with one of three ministerial phones. The minister, for whatever reason, can't answer one of the three, so the driver picks up. (Not physically, of course. Hands-free, if driving.)

The garda who picks up has to strike a note somewhere between subservient (just in case the caller is the Taoiseach) and discouraging, so that a caller egging to pass on a state secret to the minister doesn't start disgorging straight away.

Once the garda driver knows it's me, the temperature warms up and the information flows freely.

'Hasn't come out of his house yet, but give him five minutes.'

'I can see him halfway down the street, he's after getting caught with a bunch of women that are hugging him something awful.'

'She's on the other phone but she's nodding, she'll be off it in a minute.'

The point about the three-phone pass-the-mobile game that ministers play with their drivers throughout each working day is how busy it shows ministers to be. Do ministers – or indeed any other politicians – get publicly praised for working like slaves? No, they don't. Which is why the best advice to anybody thinking of going into politics is: *don't*.

Here's where I take my life in my hands. This is going to take courage. To be honest, it would be easier to confess to glue-sniffing while wearing wedgies than to make the following claims, but make them I will.

- Politicians work harder than almost anyone else in Ireland.
- Politicians work harder during their so-called holidays than almost anyone else in Ireland.

Of course exceptions exist. But for most public representatives, the summer holidays come with inverted commas around them, because they keep working. Ministers, except when they're out of the country, pitch up in their departments fairly regularly throughout the so-called summer break. But backbenchers work equally hard in the vacation months. One of the great unfairnesses of political life is that politicians get bad press for not coming back until the Dáil resumes, yet get no credit for being dragged back, well in advance of the Dáil resuming, to attend think-ins in different parts of the country. Think-ins that could be called the Electric Picnic, unplugged.

Most politicians work through the summer. Then they attend think-ins. Then they'll go back to Leinster House and get abused for having been away so long. Then they'll start worrying about the next election, and the guy from their own party who wants their seat so bad, his posterior itches at the very thought of it. When an election is called, it will give them the right to spend weeks walking their constituency taking stick from total strangers and begging those total strangers for another few years of constant media abuse.

What are they? Nuts?

The ones who survive tend to be those who have supportive mates. Gemma Hussey, former Fine Gael Minister, in her Cabinet diaries (*At the Cutting Edge*, 1990) repeatedly mentions the 'consolation' offered by phone calls with her husband, Derry. 'The family are supportive and so are a lot of other people,' she notes, early in her ministerial career.

Although Bertie Ahern's marriage broke up, one of the things that kept him afloat during difficult times was the team of largely unknown friends and supporters with whom he has the legendary pint of Bass in a Drumcondra pub at weekends. Garret Fitzgerald's late wife was not just a fierce supporter of her husband, but an intellectual equal who – it was resentfully observed by Cabinet colleagues at the time – influenced his thinking on policy at least as much as they did.

Picking a team is easier than you might think. People love to be asked to help other people. People particularly love to join conspiracies, and being part of the 'kitchen cabinet' of a prospective politician is a lot of fun. Not as much fun as being in the kitchen cabinet of an elected TD or Senator. Not nearly as much fun as serving a minister. And a quantum leap away from being part of a Taoiseach's inner circle. But, even if your man or woman isn't yet on a ticket, never mind elected, it's still flattering to be asked and enjoyable to contribute.

Politicians picking their teams should obey management consultant David Maister's advice: go for the 'people with the shining eyes'. The ones with energy. It doesn't matter if the energy leads to argument: any politician needs to have ideas kicked around in private before they advance them in public.

In addition to energy, a politician's team needs a variety of skills. Marketing. Maths. Political cop-on. Expertise in specialist areas, like the environment, the economy, fundraising, writing and education. Experience of canvassing and postering.

The meetings should be as informal as possible and as focused as possible. Never have a meeting without tasks allocated, decisions made. If you reject advice from a member of your team, go back and tell them why. Listen to your people. Thank them. Mention them to others – not necessarily as your advisers, but because of their career expertise. In other words, if you have a pensions expert on your team, then you can recommend them to businesses and individuals when the pensions issue comes up – as, these days, it frequently does.

Kitchen cabinets do not have to be paid. More to the point, they will serve you better if they are not paid. Think of the 'right arm' analogy. You don't pay your right arm. It gets a constant blood supply, messages from your brain, the challenge of being asked to learn new skills and demonstrate old ones, and a sense of belonging to something bigger than itself. Ditto with your metaphorical right arm.

At every stage in your political career, listen to advice. You don't have to take advice. You don't have to act on it. Just listen to it. Merely being listened to is one of the greatest gifts available. Adapt the Pareto rule: do 20 per cent of the talking, 80 per cent of the listening. Not all the advice you will get, even from those who love you and want the best for you, will be good. Some of the advice you will get, from those who do not love you and fervently hope that your career will wither on the vine and be decisively composted, will be bad.

Ambrose Bierce, whose wonderful *The Devil's Dictionary* (1911) should be on every politician's bookshelf, dubbed advice 'the smallest current coin', and offered a little doggerel to reinforce the point:

> 'The man was in such deep distress,'
> Said Tom, 'That I could do no less
> Than give him good advice.' Said Jim:
> 'If less could have been done for him
> I know you well enough, my son,
> To know that's what you would have done...'

Having advised politicians of all political hues for more than thirty years, I'm fascinated by the desire of the current generation to be advised a) on what cause or theme they can safely and productively espouse (as opposed to the old days, when most politicians arrived already possessed of a dream), b) on what clothes will make them look powerful, c) on what words will convey dynamism, statesmanship and whatever you're having yourself.

Listening to advice can get you onto the first rung of the ladder, but a set of core objectives and a ruthless sense of self are what will get you to the top, with or without advice. In fact, a Professor of Psychology at TCD, Michael Fitzgerald, develops in his book, *Autism and Creativity* (2004), his belief that some successful politicians, such as Éamon de Valera, suffered (or gained from) what's called 'high-functioning autism' or Asperger's Syndrome. According to Fitzgerald, Dev showed evidence of isolating behaviour and was always regarded as 'something of an outsider'.

He quotes Dr Ken Whittaker, former Secretary of the Department of Finance, who knew de Valera well, as saying that he 'had no social graces'. The implication is not that the former President had bad manners, but rather that he had a social impairment: he simply did not understand how other people were feeling at any given time and could not, as a result, respond to those feelings by easy or sensitive congeniality. The *Irish Examiner*'s T. Ryle Dwyer, referring to this odd disconnectedness, more bluntly suggested that 'if behind [deValera's] cold, impersonal countenance…there seems to be no real humanity, possibly it's because there was none.'

It helped Éamon de Valera that he had unknowingly obeyed advice given earlier in this chapter. He had picked the right wife, a partner who worked around him beautifully, not unlike the way the human body can create a bunch of capillaries to carry blood around a blocked vein. Sinéad, bean de Valera, was so warm, winning and charming in her approach that her husband's social distance often failed to register with people who met them – or, when it did register, seemed appropriate to a living symbol. Her interest in myths and fairytales complemented his mathematical focus.

Whether it's Asperger's Syndrome or hearing impairment, blindness or paraplegia, any prospective politician who suffers a disability should ignore any advice that they should go into an easier career. A nation's parliament should reflect and demonstrate its full diversity.

The most ignored piece of advice given to politicians is: 'Manage your time.' None of them do. They may have in the past, but today, most politicians are just a bundle of responsive reflexes, constantly reacting to mobile phones, e-mails, microphones and cameras. Despite Noel Dempsey's efforts to put local councillors genuinely in charge of local issues, most national politicians waste eons of time on pointless local representation.

It gets worse, the higher up the chain they go. The role of government minister has been corrupted in the last couple of decades, with the active collusion of the politicians themselves. They have become general managers of everything. Because of their desire to be seen as problem-solvers, politicians have allowed their central function to be eroded and devalued. Worse, they have collaborated in the development of a learned helplessness in many areas of public life, accepting that the buck stops with them when in fact the buck should have been dealt with at a non-political level by the managers in each sector who are paid to deal with emerging problems. So anything going wrong in the banking sector becomes the personal responsibility of the Minister for Finance, every hole in a school floor is attributed to the Minister for Education, every A&E crisis belongs to the Minister for Health.

All the political parties are equally to blame for this daft situation, because when they're in opposition, it's in their interest to portray every mistake made anywhere in the public sector as emerging from a failure in oversight by the minister, and when they're in government, they want to be seen as effective and energetic. The end result is politicians micromanaging everything very badly, being excoriated for interfering on the one hand and lambasted for failure to intervene on the other.

The light at the end of the time-management tunnel, for politicians, is the regulator. Regulators are the new big thing. Regulators get to kick ass and take names. Look crooked at a regulator and they'll revoke your licence or fine you until your bottom line trembles. They're new, they're as clean as Eliott Ness and most of them are wisely refusing the temptation to become household names. They also breed like hamsters. A couple of years back, they were few and far between. Now, they're everywhere. Clever politicians, when asked to intervene in an issue governed by a regulator, explain to the voter how to contact him or her, and stay out of that particular maelstrom.

The other piece of advice which always and ever goes unheeded, although it shouldn't, is to politicians in government parties: Don't, on radio or TV, list off the promises you have kept. Think about it. Imagine any wife coming home to her husband in the evening and saying, 'I promised you when I married you that I'd be faithful. I've been faithful the whole week.' The husband, in that situation, would not feel warm, cuddly and reassured by the claims to have delivered on promises made. None of us think that way.

Yet politicians, once they go into government, develop this mad obsession with listing off all the good things they've done. If you're thinking of going into politics, please don't do this.

When you're on radio or TV, don't ever say 'I'm glad you asked me that question' or 'I'll come to that, but first.' Answer the bloody question. Honestly. Briefly, if it puts you on a pitch you're not comfortable playing on. Link to something more interesting. And – at all times, obey the following vital, if negative, advice.

- Don't tell the interviewer their job.
- Don't tell them they shouldn't be focusing on negatives and that here you have a good news story to offer. Good news stories are a pain.
- Don't tell them media is always against your particular party.
- Don't tell them that opinion polls don't matter, and that you, personally, don't go in for beauty contests.
- Don't ask broadcast journalists questions. It wastes your time on the air.
- Don't whinge at a print journalist who's taken a pop at you. Most people have forgotten it by the next day. Including the journalist.
- Don't ever believe that because journalists like you, the public does, too. Fine Gael's Michael Noonan once observed that the biggest mistake a politician

can make on RTE's *Questions and Answers* is to believe that, because they know they're winning with the studio audience, they're winning with the broadcast audience, too. Keep your eye on the people you need to reach. And they're neither journalists nor the kind of political heads who turn up for *Q&A*.

- Don't get pally with one particular journalist. Every other hack will spot, within weeks, the source of that journalist's leaked exclusives. If you're going to leak, leak with a fair promiscuity.

- Don't put yourself in a position where you could fall asleep during a phone interview. (Never mind the name. It happened. And the station broadcast his snores.)

- Don't involve your toddlers in photo shoots. You're opening the door to later coverage of them when, hormones and attitudes raging, they get into trouble with the Gardai.

- Don't ever be photographed with a silly hat on.

- Don't ever be photographed eating. Nigella is the only person in the world who can do it and still look attractive.

Consultant, anonymous

If a politician isn't good on names, they'd better get someone close to them who is. Back in the days of the Roman Empire, Senators always had a slave called a *nomenclator* at their side. The *nomenclator*'s job was to remember names and mutter them to his owner as people came up to him, so he could flatter them by 'knowing' them. American presidents have that kind of service. Of course, several Irish male politicians have it, too. It's called their wife.

An Taoiseach, Bertie Ahern, TD

My mother's advice to me was: 'Work hard, be fair, understanding and considerate to people. Listen to the point of view of others. Then make up your mind up and be fair in your actions and decisions.'

When I was an accounts clerk, aged eighteen, working in Bord Bainne Cheantar Bhaile Átha Cliath (Dublin District Milk Board), the financial controller one day gave me a bit of advice that stayed with me: 'The work, study, effort and commitment put into the next few years will decide what you will achieve, the position you will hold, the standard of life you will have and the friends you will make.

Enda Kenny, leader of Fine Gael

My father always advised me: 'Be moving before the ball is kicked.' Meaning that you need to anticipate events and shape them, rather than just letting them happen. Lead, rather than react.

Bill Clinton

Part of the art of politics is smiling when you feel like you're swallowing a turd.

Albert Reynolds, former Taoiseach

It's not the big things that bring you down, it's the little things.

Machiavelli

A wise ruler cannot and should not keep his word when such an observance of faith would be to his disadvantage.

Always remember, if you are not going to kill, do not wound.

Adi Roche, Founder, Chernobyl Children's Project International
'Let nothing perturb you…nothing frighten you…all things pass eventually.'
Mum around the time of the 1997 presidential election.

'Never the backward glance.' From the late Huge Coveney after the same
election.

'Never let your wants exceed your needs.' Mum.

'When you are perceived to be successful, you win both false and true
friends. Succeed anyway.' Mum (but probably quoting someone else).

'Give the world the best you have, it may never be enough…but give your
best anyway. Never give up.' Mum (whenever I felt like giving up).

'Whenever you doubt yourself or your motives…go back into your heart
for the truth. It will guide you, keep you safe…keeping you true to why
you do what you do and give you the strength to do more and do it even
better.' Mum.

Molly Ivins, newspaper columnist
Clinton habitually agrees with whomever he's talking to. This is a good way
to save yourself a lot of unnecessary arguments.

Kennedy embodied that aristocratic ideal (you see it in the Peter Wimsey
character) of making excellence look easy. You're supposed to get a First
at Oxford and play championship cricket all without appearing to work for
it. With guys like Nixon, the sweat always shows.

11

Advice on Health

Advice on health has a poor track record. Medics, down the years, have got it spectacularly wrong. Not only have they got it spectacularly wrong, they have failed to deduce from the numbers of patients dying directly after a treatment that there just might have been something a bit wrong with the treatment.

Sometimes, it has to be admitted, they haven't been able to give good advice because the illness prostrating their patients arrived out of nowhere, killed within hours or days and was not amenable to any treatment. When the Black Plague hit Europe in the middle of the fourteenth century, the only preventive measure that seemed to work was to get out of the stricken city and into the hills above. Boccaccio's *Decameron* came about because of the advice to flee infection: the disease-refugees, to entertain themselves, told stories, and he gathered them into a fat volume still in print.

Nobody understood that that the plague vector was the flea, carried on infected rats coming off ships. It was noticed, however, that people in smoky homes didn't seem to be quite as vulnerable to infection as others, possibly because fleas didn't like the atmosphere. That led to some advice, remembered in a diary of the time kept by Thomas Hearn:

I have been told that in the last great plague in London none that kept tobacconist's shops in London had the plague. It is certain that smoaking was looked upon as a most excellent preservative. In so much, that even children were obliged to smoak. And I remember that I heard formerly Tom Rogers, who was the yeoman beadle, say, that when he was that year, when the plague raged, a school-boy at Eaton [*sic*], all the boys of that school were obliged to smoak in the school every morning, and that he was never whipped so much in his life as he was one morning for not smoaking.

The real difficulty about doctors in history getting it wrong is that their advice usually led to action. So, when Beethoven's doctor told him that his stomach pains could be cured by lancing and that the doctor would then put neat little bandages over the wounds, the composer, while he undoubtedly had the choice of sticking with the stomach pain, opted to go under the knife. Recent chemical analysis of his hair and bones reveal that the lead poultices applied by the doctor, post-surgery, killed him. (He was arguably luckier than Charles II, the chronicle of whose ante-mortem suffering at the hands of a number of royal physicians makes his recorded civility uniquely admirable.)

Advice, handed from one generation of doctors to the next, led to the loss of millions of litres of blood from the already sick. Bleeding cured almost everything, the way doctors told it. The more blood you could drain out of the sick person, the better. In Homer's time, for example, Dr Aretaeus, having opened a client's vein, 'allowed the blood to flow till the patient was ready to faint away.' The longevity of this practice, combined with the fact that surgeons in the middle ages were multi-skilled, doing hair-cutting as well as the day job, led to the red and white striped poles which used to identify barbers' shops. The red referred to blood. What a Unique Selling Proposition.

For more than a century, because modern medicine had become so wise, it sneered at those old barber/surgeons for doing something so stupid. Until a recent study into the possibility of a link between too much iron in the body and cardiovascular disease suggested that blood-letting might have its virtues, after all. People with too much iron in their systems can be helped by giving regular blood donations. Of course, what ailed most of the people whose blood was swiped, throughout history, was not an excess of iron, so the enthusiastic advice that they allow their barber to draw off a litre or two killed, rather than cured them.

Women having babies were subjected to probably the worst health advice ever given, and the worst treatment, similarly, once the era of the 'wise woman', who knew how to deliver babies and employ herbal remedies passed, and obstetrics became the preserve of male surgeons. They dissected the dead and brought whatever bug the dead had died of as a free gift to their pregnant female patients, killing them by infecting them with puerperal fever. Although one doctor figured out what was going wrong, he wasn't posh enough or persuasive enough to get them to change their ways. (Advice-givers often have a tough time of it, and when they fail, the rest of us can have a tough time of it as a result of their failure.)

In our own country, if you go through the older corridors of the Rotunda Hospital, you'll see elegant circular wrought-iron grates the size of wagon wheels in the floors, and half-circle matching grates over some of the doors. They're the legacy of a prestigious Master of the hospital, who advised that they be installed in order to reduce the number of deaths of women in childbirth in the hospital which, he postulated, were due to 'miasma'. Sure enough, deaths in childbirth immediately dropped at the hospital. What nobody noticed was that the midwives had decided, around the same time, that it might be more pleasant for mothers delivering their babies if they did it on a bed of fresh straw, as opposed to straw already used by a previous mother. The 'beds' got changed after each patient so that the infection-carrying straw was dumped.

It was the changed straw that did the trick, not the 'miasma' theory. But it's the miasma master whose name is recorded in framed gilt calligraphy on the walls of the hospital, not the midwife whose advice was life-saving. The moral would seem to be that if you're going to give good advice and are a woman, you may need to be born in the right century.

Even in the twentieth century, doctors gave advice on peptic ulcers which cured none of them. Eventually, one medic got the message: these things were caused by bacteria. Would they listen to him? No. So he injected the bacteria into his healthy self and hey presto: a peptic ulcer. Today, if you present with peptic ulcer symptoms, you're likely to be prescribed an antibiotic, which will clear the problem in a matter of weeks.

On the other hand, if you arrive in your doctor's surgery with a suppurating head cold, you may get huffy if he or she tells you to take Paracetemol and lots of lemon drinks, because you feel so ghastly, you're convinced you deserve an antibiotic. The GP who does not recommend an antibiotic is a good GP: the head-cold virus wouldn't recognise or pay attention to it. The GP who yields to pressure and writes out an antibiotic prescription is helping you make yourself resistant to antibiotics, and you may rue that, at some point down the line when you have a really serious bacterial infection that shrugs off the medication you receive because it got used to it long before and has worked out ways to survive it.

By the way, if you do have a head cold or flu, two bits of medical advice are worth following. The first is to go home and stay home. Quarantine yourself in the interests of the public good, rather than dragging yourself into the office to play hero/victim and in the process infect half the people you encounter. The second is to be wary of Paracetemol. Too many flu-sufferers take Panadol and then make themselves up one of those lemon drinks sold in packets which promise to reduce the symptoms of colds or flu. Of course they do. They're filled with Paracetemol. The double dose is extremely dangerous and damaging to your innards.

As this book goes to press, medical journals are filling up with studies indicating the possibility that the epidemic of obesity in the western world may have been kick-started by a virus. This is great news for the mortified overweight among us, but doesn't solve our problem. That problem is undoubtedly exacerbated by the fact that most of us feel we have to use our car and the lift to save time, even though we know that by walking we can lose weight and help the environment. Advice from the Department of Health to take regular vigorous exercise goes unheeded by the majority.

It's still good advice, and the earlier a regular habit of exercise starts, the better. Teddy Roosevelt seemed a most unpromising child. He was skinny, small, had poor eyesight and suffered from dreadful asthma attacks.

'You have the mind,' his father told him when Teddy was twelve. 'But you have not the body, and without the help of the body the mind cannot go as far as it should. You must make the body.' (You can almost hear the lad's mother in the background, can't you, saying, 'Would you leave the child alone, sure he can hardly breathe…')

Maybe because the years up to that point had been so difficult, the twelve-year-old took the advice, beginning to work out with weights, to ice-skate in the winter, to hike and hunt. In addition, he went horse-riding, rowing in boats and took to the boxing ring.

The end result was a block of sturdy energy, boundless courage and stunning self-confidence.

The man who became President also read, non-stop. When he died in his sleep, a book was found under his pillow. His vice-president maintained that death had to take him sleeping, for if Roosevelt had been awake, there would have been a fight.

Getting strong, as a kid, was undoubtedly of value to Teddy Roosevelt. But no matter how strong he got, he'd never have been able to avoid becoming infected with a childhood illness like measles, had an epidemic happened. Today, children are vaccinated early against killer diseases like measles. (If you regard measles as a minor ailment, you miss the part it played in history, when the white man in the new world gave Native Americans blankets infected with measles, because the newcomers had observed that the disease affected the 'redskins,' to whom it was brand new, much more virulently than it did white people who had built up generations of resistance to it. Blankets were a weapon of mass destruction – of biological mass destruction – long before Saddam Hussein got the notions he never turned into reality.)

Where vaccination is not given to children, as with chickenpox, the current trend is for parents to actively promote the disease. Parents of an infected child will throw a chickenpox party, advising neighbours and friends and fellow-customers at the local playgroup to bring along their kids so that every family gets it at the same time and gets over it at the same time.

Mark Twain followed this approach – and was lucky to survive. One spring, when he was twelve-and-a-half, measles struck his village, killing one child roughly every day, and paralysing the populace with 'fright, distress, despair'. Uninfected children were immured in their homes to preserve them from the illness, and because of the danger, those homes were filled with solemnity and prayer: 'the family moved spectrally about on tiptoe, in a ghostly hush.'

This imprisonment became unbearable for the youngster. He later wrote:

> Life on these miserable terms was not worth living, and at last I made up my mind to get the disease and have it over, one way or the other. I escaped from the house and went to the house of a neighbour where a playmate of mine was very ill with the malady. When the chance offered I crept into his room and got into bed with him. I was discovered by his mother and sent back into captivity. But I had the disease; they could not take that from me. I came near to dying. The whole village was interested, and anxious, and sent for news of me every day; and not only once a day, but several times. Everybody believed I would die.

He didn't, and his daft adventure turned out to have been a good career move, because his mother, thereafter, decided neither she nor school could control him and apprenticed him to a printer, where his fascination with words began. He had the grace, nonetheless, not to advise others to seek out infectious diseases and go to bed with them.

An interesting fight about medical advice happened between Florence Nightingale and a bunch of Irish nuns during the Crimean War. Nightingale promulgated cleanliness. Wounded soldiers had their dressings removed and their wounds debrided and disinfected every day. This process was painful for the patients and challenging for the nurses. Soon, another war broke out, with Nightingale essentially accusing the nuns of being lazy, filthy incompetents. The

Mother in charge of the nursing sisters withdrew their services and they took the long journey home to Ireland.

Probably cognisant of the counter-productivity of taking on the most popular and influential women in the world, the sisters kept their mouth shut about their side of the argument, except when it came to explaining to their superiors and their bishops that, while they totally agreed with and practised pristine cleanliness, they did not believe in torturing a grievously wounded man in what were self-evidently the last hours of his life by tearing bandages, adhesive with dried blood, away from already painful wounds and then scraping dead tissue away from those wounds. It was more humane, held the nuns, to spend time comforting a man while he died.

Nightingale's advice won out, for a number of reasons. She was Protestant at a time when the British powerbase was exclusively Protestant. She gathered data and used it devastatingly well, coming up with graphics that would do credit to a modern computer. She didn't care who she annoyed. (When Queen Victoria sent a message asking if bottles of eau-de-cologne would make the wards more pleasant, Florence snapped that bottles of gin would be much more effective.)

Bad medical advice – and treatment – is accepted and has always been accepted because the patient believes in the adviser. A medieval commentator named Galen remarked: 'He cures most successfully in whom the people have the most confidence.'

The converse also happens. A lethally bad doctor, giving useless advice or therapy, can damage enormous numbers of people because his charm, or in some cases his sheer bullying authority draws a disproportionate number of willing patients to him or her.

Sidney Poitier, actor

I've wrestled with questions about my father's character in part because I'm still wrestling with my own. And that battle has taught me that if the image one holds of one's self contains elements that don't square with reality, one is best advised to let go of them, however difficult that may be.

A few years ago I was required to undergo surgery for prostate cancer. In the weeks before surgery my most important concern was waking up cancer-free, but a close second was preserving my image. I hate like hell to admit any weakness or failure. What would the press say if the prognosis was poor?

But surgery left me naked to myself and to the world, with prostate and camouflage removed. Shortcomings, weaknesses, frailties, vulnerabilities, inadequacies, self-doubts, and all – my total reality in plain sight. No less flawed than most, and no longer burdened by the need to appear otherwise.

At every point through all the years before, the greatest threat to my life's program had been my fear of failure. Not failure itself, but my fear of failure. And now, once the surgery had been scheduled, I managed to translate the publicity that I knew would result into a full-scale, worldwide failure thing. I had enjoyed so many successes over the years that my lifelong fear of failure had been relegated to the sub-basement. But it had remained alive and well down there, ready to come out with a roar with the cancer diagnosis. With blunt honesty my cancer said, 'You're not a 'star'; you're a human being, vulnerable like all the rest.'

12

ADVICE ON FEAR

Most advice offered on fear wastes the time of the advice-giver and receiver equally. Counselling someone not to panic when they're in a situation which makes them panic is so idiotic, it's a miracle the advice-givers don't get clouted for it. They get off scot-free because the panicker is too focused on terror to worry about, or deal with, some moron on the sidelines burbling about staying calm, and after the panic is over, the panicker is too ashamed of having lost control to hit the advice-giver when that person, smug smile affixed to face, murmurs, 'Didn't I tell you?'

The shape and sharpness of fear is unique to the person experiencing it, as most of us discover when we're toddlers and the doctor approaches with a syringe.

'This won't hurt at all,' they say. Or, more honestly, 'You'll feel a little pinch.'

'A little pinch' is not what you felt, as a two-year old, when the doctor stuck that needle in you. You knew a stabbing when you experienced it. And from then on, you knew that life's terrors were tougher on you than on the people ever-willing to give you advice on how to cope with them.

The medieval warrior and ruler Castruccio Castracani of Lucca had this down pat. When he was sailing from Pisa to Livorno on one occasion, a storm broke out to make the journey more interesting. Castruccio was terrified. Too terrified to pretend not to be terrified. He was good and visibly panicked. One of his entourage decided to patronise him by announcing that he wasn't afraid of anything.

'I don't wonder at that,' Castruccio snapped. 'Each man values his life for what it is worth.'

Telling a child not to be afraid of the dark, that nothing will happen and that Mammy and Daddy are downstairs, is nearly as insensitive as announcing that, in the same situation, you wouldn't be one bit scared. You're bigger than the kid, more experienced than the kid and aren't going to be on your own, aged four, in the kid's room.

This entire chunk of advice misses the point of children's fears: that they have nothing to do with fact or reality. When children were asked recently about dangers on the roads, for example, they instantly named them. Lions. Tigers. Dragons. Boyracers and DUI maniacs didn't figure. The children had no experience of the last two. Admittedly, any lion, tiger or dragon experience they had was vicarious, unless their parents worked at the zoo and had problems finding good childcare. But the children simply populated the roads with the most frightening figures they'd encountered.

Growing up is supposed to remove fear from us. It doesn't. Just as facial expressions carry the same meaning in countries and cultures all over the world, so adult fears, according to psychological research, are fairly common among grown-ups, no matter where they come from. Most adults are afraid of one or more of the following:

- Public speaking
- Heights
- Insects

- Money problems
- Death
- Illness
- Deep water
- Loneliness
- Flying
- Dogs

Going to the dentist used to be a big fear, but since fluoride was introduced into water supplies, the childhood trauma inflicted by dentists has reduced and the fear has fallen off most adult lists. If humans were logical, the fear of flying would have fallen off the lists, too, since air travel has become safer and safer over the past half-century, but fear of flying seems to be stickier than fear of the drill.

The order of adult terrors changes, depending on factors and location. But public speaking tends to stay right up there at the top. (For the best possible advice on that, buy a copy of *Talk the Talk*: *How to Say What you Want to Say*.)

Fear is a good thing. In fact, fear is an essential survival mechanism. Pour enough alcohol into twenty-year-old drivers, and their fear of being killed on the road tends to diminish. Of course, their chances of being killed on the road, if they get behind the wheel of a car in that condition, greatly increase.

In normal people, when a frightening stimulus presents itself, the brain responds by asking questions: How bad is this? Will it eat me? Can I fight it? An unprecedented challenge, though, may cause panic, which is fear on steroids. It may shut down the reasoning process, leaving an almond-shaped structure deep in the brain called the amygdala to take over.

There's no reasoning with the old 'reptile brain' and no advice that can make it see sense. It's almost as if the person has no free will: panic takes over and they freeze. This inability to process advice or even pre-existing knowledge in the face of terror is why some passengers in a downed plane sit passively, rather than rushing to the emergency exit and flinging themselves down the escape chutes before fire engulfs the fuselage, whereas others step over and beyond them to preserve themselves.

Panic is a kind of shut-down, where reasoning goes AWOL and all that's left is hyperventilation, heart palpitation, cold sweats, shaking hands and paralysis. People who know they panic in a certain situation may choose a lifestyle that obviates the possibility of their encountering that fear stimulus. When a fear becomes a constant worrying issue, it's an anxiety. When an anxiety turns into a life-limiting, disabling constraint, it's called a phobia.

One of the most common phobias is aviaphobia, or fear of flying. Confident and otherwise competent people who suffer aviaphobia simply will not fly, because the prospect of being taken in an aluminium tube 30,000 feet in the air chills their soul. They are sure that if the plane had an emergency, they would neither cope nor survive. It's a lot simpler – at least within Ireland – to use the train. Some aviaphobics force themselves to go on occasional flights for work or family reasons, but do it heavily medicated, using Zoloft or alcohol.

People afraid of heights don't buy penthouses, no matter what advice they get from the real-estate guy. People terrified of lifts improve their health by walking up seven or eight flights of stairs. (For seriously good advice about elevators, next time you're in a multi-storey building, take a look at the little notice near the call buttons of the ground-floor lift entrance: In the Event of Fire, Do not Use Elevator. Just one of the reasons is that in one horrific incident in the US, a firefighter wanting to get higher up in a skyscraper where fire had engulfed one floor jumped into the elevator, only to be brought to the fire-floor itself. The electronics responded to the heat, bringing the lift to the one floor the firefighter didn't want to be on, the doors opened and the man died.)

Unfortunately, not all fear stimuli are avoidable. A friend of mine, terrified of bridges, has to be gently talked across any bridge by her teenage son. She finds bridges that are much trafficked and flat less threatening than great soaring multi-spanned jobs, but if she could manage, she'd stay on Dublin's southside and never cross a river, ascend in an elevator or take to the skies. Short of changing careers, however, she's stuck doing all three, now and then.

Another friend is terrified of birds. All birds. On holiday, she won't go near a nature reserve or out on a boat if a bird is likely to land on it. If she enters your home and discovers you own a budgie, she's back out the door quicker than it can say 'Who's a pretty phobic, then?'

We call other people's fears 'phobias' and tell them either to get over them or to get treatment for them. Because phobia-ownership is no fun, when they fail to get over them, they frequently do get treatment for them. Sometimes it works. Sometimes it doesn't. I know one man who has done every fear of flying course available. He still won't fly. People advising him to get over his irrational fears have quoted pilots who announce, when the plane lands, 'The safest part of your journey is over. Drive home safely,' because pilots know their passengers stand a greater chance of being killed driving the few miles from the airport than they did in a 3,000 mile journey across the Atlantic.

Since passengers first began to travel by plane, nearly a hundred years ago, fewer than 14,000 of them have lost their lives in airplane disasters. One in about four million is the average person's chance of dying in an plane crash. But that doesn't stop most of us curling up our toes as the plane lashes along the runway, willing it into the air and releasing our breath only when take-off is complete.

I'm not sure there are programmes to rid people of the dread of elevators or bridges, but if they were, they would undoubtedly take the form of gentle, gradual exposure to the fear inducer, because that's ultimately the shape taken by programmes designed to reduce panic attacks in the face of predictable challenges. Someone who has a spider phobia may be asked to think and talk about spiders first, then view pictures of spiders, then gradually get to the point where they can touch a spider, all the time, at least in theory, reducing the panic that builds up inside them at the very mention of an arachnid.

The best advice anybody could give to someone who is naturally fearful is: 'Turn off the telly.' Research indicates that 'shut-ins,' people who, through illness or age don't tend to have much in the way of social networks and contacts, tend to watch a lot of television to fill in their times spent at home, and, as a direct result, have a greatly, even grossly swollen perception of the dangers outside. Because they see all the bad stuff like fires, bombings, car crashes and scaffolding collapses on the TV, and because one programme after another deals with child abuse, infectious illness and the perils of A&E, they believe the streets are teeming with child molesters and predatory bugs, just waiting to latch on to them and put them on a trolley in Casualty.

Psychologists call this the availability heuristic. The availability heuristic is the one that makes us figure a threat is enormous, simply because it comes to mind immediately. So if media has been barking on about the possibility of avian flu transferring to the feline population, the person whose main source of information is the telly begins to look dubiously at Snowball, the family tabby, especially if she sneezes. Don't miaow at me, you killer...

In the same way, if media is running stories about overcrowding in A&E, with accounts by individuals of their suffering at the hands of a particular hospital or ward, the Minister for Health may issue factual advice saying that the overwhelming majority of the citizenry who come in contact with the healthcare system are happy as clams with the treatment they get, but that advice will not outweigh the impact of the individual emotional story seen on last night's television news. The minister's research-based, evidence-based comments will be dismissed as 'just statistics' or more directly, as lies.

Once a fear has been implanted in the human mind, advice suggesting that the frightened response may be out of kilter with the reality rarely makes anybody feel more confident. Whenever newspapers suggest that gangs are out there waiting to mow you down with a sub-machine gun, that drug-peddling battalions cluster around the school gate seeking to flog crack to your kid or that your chances of being mugged in the street are high, people become terrified of 'the crime wave'.

Eighty years ago, an American journalist named Lincoln Steffens sniggered at the 'crime waves' of his own time. He wrote:

> Every now and then, there occurs the phenomenon called a crime wave. New York has such waves periodically. They sweep over the public and nearly drown the lawyers, judges, preachers and other leading citizens who feel they must explain and cure these extraordinary outbreaks of lawlessness. I enjoy crime waves. I made one once.

What happened was that Steffens reported on a burglary at a Wall Street brokerage business. Another well-known journalist on another paper got yelled at the following day for being scooped by Steffens. He went out and drummed up his very own burglary, which in turn infuriated Steffens's editor. In no time at all, the two journalists, followed by dozens of others, were practically begging criminals to do their worst at a time and place favouring one hack or another. What the pressmen were actually doing was highlighting crimes that happened all the time but hadn't been paid much attention to until the competition between the two big newspapers started. The police commissioner hauled the two main proponents of the 'crime wave' into his office and told them to get a grip, proving factually that, while coverage of crime had gone up, crime itself was at more or less the same level it had always been at.

Telling you all that, if you believe your locality is filled with muggers, rapists and druggies, may be good advice, but it is unlikely to be terribly effective. On the other hand, advising you to go and take a Te Kwan Do course or a programme in self-defence or kick-boxing, could be markedly effective. Giving people something to do when they are afraid is one of the most effective ways of helping them cope with their fear: hence the way anaesthetists ask patients undergoing a general anaesthetic to count backwards from ten as the sedation is about to be administered. It keeps the patient occupied.

The same principle is behind advice given in songs like the one from *The King and I*, promulgating self-distraction as a method of coping with terror:

> Whenever I feel afraid,
> I hold my head up high
> And whistle a happy tune
> So no-one ever knows
> I'm afraid.

How effective the whistling is depends on the depth of the dread. George Eliot said that music could help with every emotion – other than the extremes of fear and guilt. The Polar explorer Shackleton, recognising the importance of music to the maintenance of morale in a terrifying situation, ordered his men to rid themselves of all accoutrements, personal and otherwise, in order to survive the trek across the ice towards rescue, but made an exception of the banjo owned by one them. Music, he knew, was a major supporter of morale.

The old advice not to fear the darkness but to light a candle, similarly, has a lot going for it. The fear of darkness is primeval. Death and darkness are closely related. Darkness often serves as a metaphor for death. But the fear of the dark is not just an irrationality related to mortality. It's also a race memory related to crime. When Sir Robert Peel set out to create a modern police force, one of the most effective actions he took was to improve lighting in cities at night. Crime – like the cockroach – prefers the dark, and so the level of muggings reduced. (Lamps in Dublin, as late as 1783, were so far apart that one visitor said the only good they served was to show the 'danger of falling into a cellar'.)

The other logical, rational reason for fear of the dark may be rooted in worker-exploitation. Trying to work in the dark, or with the darkness mitigated only by a candle, is bad for your eyes, which is why, from the twelfth century onwards, English craft guilds banned nightwork. At around the same time, albeit for a slightly different reason, the *French Book of Trades* warned gold and silversmiths against working once the natural light had failed, for 'light at night is insufficient for them to ply their trade well and truly'. An old sexist proverb warned: 'Choose not a woman, nor linen clothe by the candle.' Although we do much less talking these days about ghosts and ghouls and things that go bump in the night, fear of the dark never seems to leave the human psyche.

One of the most interesting writers about fear is a man named Gavin de Becker, who earns his living by protecting people against kidnapping and similar crimes:

> Intuition has many messengers, but the clearest and most urgent is fear. Nothing in life gets attention as reliably as fear – and that's the way the system is designed to work. Fear does some miraculous things when we perceive that we are in the presence of danger. First, it gets our bodies ready for action with a dose of adrenaline. It heats up the lactic acid in our muscles for running or fighting, and it even gives us a chemical called cortisol that makes our blood clot more quickly in case we're cut in a fight.

Gavin de Becker's excellent books of advice stress that 'intuition is knowing without knowing why, knowing even when you can't see the evidence.' He warns against overriding an apparently irrational fear, explaining that it may be based on evidence you are not able to process consciously. But the evidence is there, and with the evidence, the threat. His advice is to take apparently irrational fears seriously, because they are likely to be founded on half-seen evidence.

Horace, Roman poet
A good scare is worth more than any advice.

Mary Schiavo, pilot and former Inspector General of the US Department of Transportation
I and a host of other passengers already carry our own smoke hoods, because those little oxygen masks that are supposed to fall from the

ceiling do nothing to protect passengers from smoke or toxic fumes in the cabin. (Not to mention that you cannot get up and run through fumes and smoke to exit the plane if you are tied to the ceiling of the plane.)

…If there is an emergency, flight attendants are supposed to hand out infant life vests. As much as I admire and respect flight attendants, I would rather not rely on them to remember in the midst of a crisis that there might be one or two babies on board who need special gear. That is why, when I fly on a long trip over water with my young children, I always ask the flight attendant to let me keep the baby life vest at my seat until we land. Flight attendants have frequently balked at this request (often telling me they would get in trouble) but there is no regulation against a parent taking responsibility for the infant life vest.

Sean Kelly, Irish Institute of Sport
The best advice I ever got was, 'Keep your shirt on.' My uncle, God be good to him, was a parish priest, and when people would be getting excited and threatening to lose the head, he'd say, 'Now, hold on, hold on, keep your shirt on.' It was very good advice and has been very useful to me.

13

ADVICE ON HOLIDAYS

When, in 2005, Hurricane Katrina made bits of New Orleans, it scattered a community to the four winds and devastated a local economy. It also ruined a great tourist destination.

It could not be rebuilt for years, said the pessimists, and even if it were, could be written off as a tourist attraction, long-term. In the short-term, of course, nobody in their right mind with money in their pocket and a week or fortnight's free time was going to spend it in a semi-abandoned city, its buildings swathed, its jazz replaced by the sound of pneumatic drills and lump hammers.

The pessimists reckoned without one oddity of the human condition: we love disaster. Even when we're on our way to work, we'll slow down to gawk at two cars buried up to the crank shaft in each other. We might not want to pay for the privilege, but if you look at the huffy faces drivers develop when they are told by the Gardai to 'move along, there, now,' you can't help but wonder if – given the choice – some of them would stump up a few euro to be allowed to stay and gawk.

Disaster-tourism turned all those expectations upside down. First of all, disaster-tourism brought international gawkers to the areas devastated by the 2004 Indian Ocean tsunami as soon as the waters and the camera crews retreated. They kept coming, thereafter.

Within months of the New Orleans hurricane, daily bus tours for visitors had been reinstated, catering for passengers eager not just to see what was left of the place, but to see the damage done by the muddy waters.

The gawker instinct has created a new kind of holiday advice: 'Come and tour the disaster area you saw on TV.' The New Orleans taxi people, at first surprised to see their business picking up, have now seen it develop to such an extent that some of them have bought extra cars and trained sub-contracted drivers to run tours, so that tourists get to see where the levées broke and the river came ashore, where the natives were rounded up and sheltered, and where some of the more gruesome events of the flooding took place.

Or maybe it's not such new holiday advice. The vicarious thrill of visiting the site of someone else's tragedy has always been central to tourism. Trans-Atlantic tourism, pioneered by the Thomas Cook agency, took British travellers on tours of American Civil War battlefields within months of the end of the conflict, when it was still possible to pick up abandoned guns, clothing and other souvenirs from the torn-up soil. Mark Twain wrote:

> By some subtle law, all tragic human experiences gain in pathos by the perspective of time. We realise this in Naples when we stand musing over the poor Pompeian mother, lost in the historic storm of volcanic ashes eighteen centuries ago, who lies with her child gripped close to her breast, trying to save it, and whose despair and grief have been preserved for us by the fiery envelope which took her life but eternalised her form and features. She moves us, she haunts us, she stays in our thoughts for many days, we do not know why, for she is nothing to us, she has been nothing to any one

for eighteen centuries, whereas of the like case today
we should say 'Poor thing! It is pitiful,' and forget it in
an hour.

In order to create the silence and peace which would allow all visitors
to enjoy an historic tourist attraction, some of those attractions are
now putting up signs banning mobile phones. Now why, you ask
yourself, would any tourist bring a mobile phone into the Sistine
Chapel? Or the caves at Lascaux? Or Pompeii?

The short answer is: the holiday-maker who doesn't know how
to take a holiday. In banking, the axiom was always: 'Beware the
person who doesn't take their annual leave.' Because it was assumed
that the only reason someone would stay at work was to conceal the
fact that they might have got some of the bank's money mixed up
with their own cash.

Technology, however, has created a swatch of people who
simply take their work and their office with them when vacation
time comes around. It's the electronic abolition of the traditional
summer holiday.

Take the woman I observed on the white sands of an island
off Florida recently, in glorious sunshine. All the other tourists
were either in the sea, stretched on the sand, or systematically
selecting shells to take home with them. The woman walking at
the water's edge, however, was mostly focused on her mobile phone
conversation. Sometimes she'd stop, the waves dribbling over her
bare feet, and concentrate, her hand shielding her closed eyes as
she tried to visualise what the person on the other line was talking
about. Sometimes she'd gesture, as if her auditors were in front of
her. Phrases floated past, truncated by the shouts of children and
the crunch on sand of arriving cars.

'Impact of cost-cutting,' was one of those phrases. 'The figures from Hutchens, Kansas. They need to be worked up,' was another.

Other than improving her chances of cancer (not only was she exposed to the roasting tropical sun, but she was smoking a cigarette) this woman's holiday wasn't calculated to refresh her or allow her to take a longer view of her daily reality.

It could be suggested that a form of survivor's guilt applies to holidays in the twenty-first century. Up to this century, holidays were fastened on as deserved and welcome opportunities to have a great break. In this century, we don't feel they're deserved and we're not sure we can afford to take a lengthy break: maybe they'll find out, back at the ranch, that we're expendable. Technology, that great time-saver, ensures that the best-paid people in the most responsible jobs work harder than did their counterparts in any previous century. According to anthropologist Margaret Visser:

> If we compare our employment patterns with the workday of a hunter-gatherer in the Peruvian forests (three to four hours), the average work week in pre-revolutionary France (four days), or the annual number of work-free days in fourth-century Rome (a hundred and seventy-five), we seem a very hard-driven lot.

Good advice for anybody who wants to take a real holiday is to leave the computer and the mobile phone at home. And if that bit of advice causes your hands to tremble and your head to shake in refusal, think about the possibility that you may be addicted to the tether that ties you to the office, unable to wean yourself off the constant meaningless communications it delivers.

Another counter-intuitive piece of advice about holidays concerns the camera: leave it at home. Unless you are the reincarnation of Karsh of Ottawa, you're not going to take a picture of the Eiffel Tower, the sunset over Naples or the snow in Red Square that equals any of the pictures commercially available.

Indeed, French novelist Stendhal advised tourists not even to buy pictures 'of fine views and prospects seen on one's travels, since before very long they will displace our memories completely, indeed one might say they destroy them.'

He had a point. The photographs or video disc of a significant life-event can take over from the real memory of that event. Good advice on holiday pictures, therefore?

- Don't be a pain in the ass on a tour with your picture-taking.
- Don't be a pain in the ass afterwards with your picture-showing.
- Don't spend so much time going through your pictures that you fail to remember the emotional totality of which they are but a physical snapshot in time.

But what if the photographs of you, after your holiday, demonstrate that you look startlingly improved by the break? That's the reality for an increasing number of Irish people who are taking cosmetic surgery vacations. A relatively recent option, it is now being heavily promoted by plastic surgeons in popular cosmetic surgery Meccas like Florida, South Africa and Costa Rica.

If you've thought of a face-lift or some other plastic surgery, you might have assumed you'd have to undergo the procedure at home, especially if you expect that any plastic surgery is going to leave you looking as if you had a head-on argument with a Harley and lost.

'But surely you have to hide for quite a while after something like a face-lift?' is the most frequently-asked-question.

First bit of advice, from a cosmetic surgery junkie? No, you don't.

Now, let's be clear. The day after a face-lift, you look as if someone inserted your face in the middle of a car tyre instead of the hub cap and inflated it. Your face, I mean. You have this huge white pneumatic bandage tied around your chin and ears, meeting above your forehead in a ceremonial bow tie. Your tissues, in reaction to the major trauma inflicted on them, swell to at least twice their normal size, no matter how frequently you apply bags of frozen peas. (Frozen peas are great for cooling down inflamed tissue, because they fit so neatly around it.) In addition, you may have drains coming out from your hairline at the back. We won't even discuss the blood clots in your hair. You look in the mirror (assuming you can open your eyes, which is difficult, because the swollen flesh around them tends to reduce them to slits) and wonder what possessed you to do what you've just done, and will you ever look like a human again.

But, three days later, the swelling has reduced, so you can open your eyes, the pneumatic bandage is gone, the drains have been pulled and your hair has been gently washed. When you look in the mirror, you see a strange moon-face with stitches at the ears and bruising beginning to spread. If you went into work or dropped in to see your mother, the resultant shock and awe would be enormous. But you're in Naples, Florida. Or a city in South Africa. Or close to a cosmetic surgery clinic in Poland. None of the people who live there know what you usually look like. For all they know, moon-face is your permanent condition and you always wear a lot of make up. The makeup conceals the bruising, you pull a scarf or a flopping sun hat over the stitches and the wound, and what's to stop you doing a little shopping or sitting on the terrace with a good book?

Three days after I had a face-lift, I went to a local bookshop and confirmed one of life's great truths in the process: people are always more interested in themselves than they are in you. I told the cashier I liked her necklace. She was chuffed and told me its history. Between looking down at her own jewellery and dealing with the books I'd bought, the credit card I presented to pay for them, the receipts, the bags and all the other minutiae, she would have been hard put to describe me ten minutes after I left the shop. She glanced at me once or twice – but had no earlier image of me to measure the present one against. Face-lift? What?

In some of the favourite cosmetic surgery locations, such as Fort Myers on the Gulf Coast of Florida, this kind of procedure is so common that locals, seeing someone in a shady hat, muffled slightly in a gauze scarf or wearing a bandage, practically go, 'Oh, you had Something Done.' Nobody stops in the street and stares. It's normal.

Of course you're not going to go horse-riding a few days after a face-lift, any more than you're going to go swimming the same week you have a breast-lift or a tummy-tuck, or using free weights directly following an arm-lift. But unless your idea of a holiday involves trekking the Himalayas or running the Boston Marathon, having plastic surgery at the beginning of your vacation allows you to have a great break thereafter, while ensuring that by the time you go back to work, a genuine holiday has happened, can be talked about and – if you want to keep your surgery secret – can be used to explain your rested and refreshed appearance..

Take Florida, for example. And let's say you want to have your eye-bag-removal or brow-lift the minute you arrive and then have your holiday. Here's the typical pattern.

First of all, there's not a snowball's chance in hell that you'll get the surgery when you're fresh off the plane from Ireland. Not from a reputable surgeon, anyway. They have to do blood tests and check that you understand all the implications and risks of what you're about to undergo. Some even do tests to ensure you're not a smoker, since smoking not only wrecks your skin, delivering 'purse-string lips' among other problems, but also complicates how your lungs cope with anaesthesia and slows your healing thereafter. It's not worth their while to waste their scalpel artistry on a heavy smoker who may become seriously ill after the operation. They want you to quit for at least six weeks before they lay a glove on you.

All these restrictions don't apply to the more minor procedures, like Botox or injection of fillers. You may have tiny blood spots on your face indicating where the Botox went in – and a good Botox doctor will tend to deliver as many as a hundred tiny injections, rather than four or five whoppers. You may have swelling from the injection of fillers, together with numbness from the kind of local anaesthetic a dentist administers. But you can leave the clinic without having to take a taxi or involve a friend.

Variations on liposuction, however, require enough anaesthesia for good practitioners to want reassurance that you will not drive for twenty-four hours afterwards, no matter how well you feel.

You're likely to have any serious surgery in a dedicated operating theatre on the doctor's premises, emerging from the general anaesthetic or the lighter 'twilight anaesthesia' in an adjoining recovery room. When they've got you lucid, removed the drips, checked your blood pressure and are satisfied you are doing well, they will release you to the care of a friend, a partner or a hired nurse, and you will go back to your hotel room or apartment, where you'll sleep a lot. You'll be brought back to the surgeon for checking the following morning, at which point bandages will be changed and (probably) reduced, you'll be briefed on wound care and given a rake of telephone numbers to ring if anything happens that puzzles or bothers you.

In a worst-case scenario, if complications ensue, you will be taken into a hospital where the surgeon has admitting rights. However, if you're a non-smoker and reasonably fit, complications are unlikely. The only complication I ever had, after a multiplicity of cosmetic surgery procedures, was serious vomiting for ten hours. It wasn't fun, and I learned to specify that a particular kind of anaesthesia must not be used on me.

I lie. I had one other complication after several procedures. A headache so bad, it was like someone had replaced my brain with a boiled cannonball. I assumed it came with the territory, until a nurse practitioner asked me, before a later procedure, how I felt once I became conscious. I mentioned the headache.

'Oh, you're a coffee-addict,' she said cheerfully.

I nodded, guiltily.

'No problem,' she said. 'We'll put caffeine in your drip.'

She did. No headache. Wondrous.

But – worst scenario – let's assume you have a more serious complication than caffeine-withdrawal, and need to be admitted to a hospital. Double-check before agreeing to any surgery on a doctor's premises that he or she has admittance rights.

Double-check the surgeon's qualifications, too. In the US, it is possible to do plastic surgery without being a board-certified plastic surgeon, but you would be out of your mind to let a physician with notions near your precious face.

If you want to keep your surgery a secret and therefore don't want to ask a friend, you'll want to hire a nurse to take care of you in your hotel or villa after the operation. Reputable surgeons maintain that you should not be on your own for even five minutes for the forty-eight hours after major surgery. Your balance may be off, and a fall could be disastrous. In all the 'cosmetic surgery countries' the clinics providing the surgery will also provide you with names of accredited nurses or nurse-practitioners with lots of expertise in taking care of post-operative patients.

Secrecy doesn't always have to be total. Two or three girlfriends may decide to take a plastic surgery holiday, with one having surgery and being cared for by the others, then switching role to carer as the others undergo the knife or the laser.

If you decide to take a plastic surgery holiday, here's the most important advice: make sure the surgeon has the highest qualifications, whether European, or, if you plan to go Stateside or to Costa Rica, those relevant there. Be obsessive about your research. Remember, a holiday can be taken lightly. A holiday which could adversely affect your face or your survival needs to be taken very seriously.

Advice about holiday health can save you a lot of misery. Take the 'airplane cold'. Professor Martin B. Hocking and a team at the University of Victoria, Canada recently set out to test the validity of the belief, held by many air travellers, that every time they go on a long-haul flight, they get a cold. The Canadian team found that the myth was fact: 'air travel increases susceptibility to upper respiratory tract infections'. On the other hand, they found that the general belief that these colds are due to recirculated air in the cabin is incorrect: 'However, a higher than normal viral load is likely to be experienced by aircraft passengers and cabin crew as a consequence of the much lower rate of outside air ventilation per person in modern aircraft than for any other ground level or transport public space.'

Six of one, half a dozen of the other, the sniffling layperson may feel. The point is that a fully loaded plane puts more people closer to each other than any other form of transport. It sure as hell puts more people closer to each other than does any home or office. In addition, the air in a plane has markedly less humidity than most normal situations. To help your immune system fight off the bugs in this dried-out atmosphere, the advice is to sip water throughout the flight.

The advice given in hospitals to help constrain the onward march of MRSA applies on a plane. Wash your hands every time you go to the loo. Carry anti-bacterial gel or antiseptic hand wipes and use them throughout the flight. Hands that touch armrests or door handles already touched by someone infected with a cold are the most efficient way of transferring the bugs to your mouth and nose. Using a mouthwash may also help.

An airplane cold is nothing compared to a gastro-intestinal virus. You can get them on land, unless you follow the advice to brush your teeth with bottled water, avoid food cooked on the street, and eat cooked, rather than raw meals. You can also get them at sea: even the poshest liners have found themselves with passengers whose symptoms could not be explained by the rise and fall of the waves. America's Centre for Disease Control provides information on its website about the track record of cruise liners when it comes to nasties like the norovirus. They don't actually advice prospective passengers to steer clear of the cruise-providers who frequently provide more than cruises, but if you want to avoid being quarantined in your cabin with the most god-awful symptoms in the world, you clearly shouldn't travel with cruise operators who do not seem to be able to keep their vessels clean and virus-free.

The advantage a cruise has is that it reduces the possibility of jet lag. The length of the flight has nothing to do with jet lag. North–south flights, for example, generate little jet lag. What matters is the number of time zones crossed, particularly west to east.

Good advice on preventing jet lag starts with adjusting your bedtime in advance of the flight. Let's say you're holidaying in the US. Four or five days before your flight back to Ireland, start going to bed an hour earlier and getting up an hour earlier in the morning.

Cut back or eliminate your use of alcohol and caffeine.

Some frequent travellers swear by two products available in overseas healthfood stores: L-tryptophan and melatonin. The first was taken off the market for almost ten years after a batch of tainted product from Japan killed several people, but has now returned. The two preparations, in different ways, help to adjust a confused body clock. However, each – particularly melatonin – can have side-effects, particularly when combined with other drugs, so ask your doctor before you experiment with either.

Arriving home from holiday with an airplane cold complicated by jet lag is now and again exacerbated by loss of your luggage. For the most part, the luggage turns up within forty-eight hours, although enough luggage goes permanently missing and unclaimed for a massive store in Atlanta to buy up and re-sell cases and their contents. To minimise the misery of lost luggage, seasoned travellers offer the following advice.

- Never put key medications in checked luggage.
- Keep a list of what's in the bag – particularly anything of value.
- Be able to describe the case accurately.
- Put more than one owner-label on the outside of the case, and put one inside the case.
- Buy unusual cases and tie bright ribbons around the handle to prevent someone inadvertently picking your case off the conveyor belt in mistake for their own.

Padhraic Ó Ciardha, leasphríomhcheannasaí, TG4
'Take the road through the mountains – you can go through Galway city any time.' Petrol attendant in Cong when I wondered whether I was being foolish in driving through a misty Maam valley go get to work.

Norman Newcombe, marketing expert

If you buy more than you planned to buy on a trip to the US, don't invest in a brand new suitcase. Visit a thrift shop. St. Vincent de Paul, Goodwill and other thrift shops always have suitcases for sale, and you can pick up a serviceable case for those extra purchases for as little as five dollars.

14

ADVICE ON APPEARANCE

Here's the time to make a confession.

For several years, I earned my living telling other people what they should wear, how they should take care of their skin, make up their faces and do their hair.

Shameful, isn't it? I started at seventeen, when Mary Kenny, then Women's Editor of the now defunct *Irish Press*, hired me as fashion and beauty correspondent. I knew nothing about either and it showed.

'I don't need someone who knows things,' she said airily. 'People who know about fashion and beauty write boring features. I want you to be funny about fashion.'

I was so funny about fashion, I got barred from the annual collection of one of the major Irish designers of the time. But, while being dismissive and smartarse about style, I nonetheless earwigged shamelessly at every gathering of women journalists. At that time, the formidable group which moved from reception to reception included Terry Keane, who never stopped going on about the importance of owning an undecorated black dress. Since I'd spent the previous ten years in an undecorated black dress called a school uniform, I passed on that guidance. Just as I passed on the advice of the then editor of a women's magazine, who, when she discovered I didn't drink wine, told me the way to make it palatable was to put six spoons of sugar in each glass and stir vigorously. Since I was sixteen stone at the time, I figured this directive might have a downside, quite apart from the fact that alcohol made me sleepy and affectionate, which is not the condition you needed to be in to survive the fashion world.

The staple advice that group constantly dispensed included the following.

- Go to a good store like Arnotts or Brown Thomas and be fitted for a bra, because 80 per cent of women wear bras that don't fit them properly. (I never obeyed this one. Communal changing rooms were bad enough. An expert horsing my boobs into an appropriate bra? Forget it.)
- Always buy one classic item you can't afford each season. A tailored jacket can pull together and put a fine gloss on a series of lesser garments.
- Buy great handbags and take care of the leather. (The only handbag I ever owned was the one I bought for my going-away outfit. Handbags are a badge of servitude, filled with childcare items and irrelevancies.)
- Own an Hermès silk scarf and you'll look like Grace Kelly. (What a load of BS.)
- Never wear silver and gold together. (Like I had that challenge. My jewellery consisted of six plastic bracelets held together by rubberised string.)
- Always make up your face while in your underwear and put a scarf over your head to prevent it getting on your clothes when you put them on.

- To be a fashion correspondent requires you to ignore one of the great pieces of advice, frequently delivered by those who never follow it to those who never will follow it: 'Don't judge a book by its cover.'

Which, on the face of it, is loopy. Bookshops would be immeasurably duller if all books had the same cover. Plus, writers like me would not be able to turn – as we always do – to the back of the wraparound, or to the fold-over flap, in order to look at the author's picture and annoy ourselves with how much younger they look than we do or how much more credibly literary.

People get crucial buying information from the cover of a book and are heavily influenced by it. One author, whose self-published paperback was carried by perhaps half a dozen local outlets, discovered he could treble his sales by simply sticking a gold sticker to the front of the book, drawing attention to a minor award it had won.

The same is true of appearance. We may piously claim to be immune to looks, and to have marvellous insight into the essence of a personality, but we're kidding ourselves. Very good-looking people tend to end up married to other very good-looking people. There's a pecking order in mating, just as there is in everything else in the animal kingdom.

There's a great scene in *The Devil Wears Prada* where Anne Hathaway, the new recruit to fashion diva Meryl Streep's magazine, sniggers at the seriousness with which her new boss considers a belt. Streep does a devastating monologue, in the course of which she establishes that while Hathaway may persuade herself that she is in some way immune to the influence of great fashion designers, even her appalling acrylic jumper belongs in a stream-of-design-consciousness originated elsewhere several years before.

Streep's character is right. As a fashion correspondent, reading *Women's Wear Daily* in order to find out whether Prince of Wales check or polka dots were the new essential, I was struck by how self-deceiving people were about what they wore. While some happily obeyed what the fashion magazines decreed, others regarded wardrobe as irrelevant to the reality of their lives.

In fact, apparel can be just as important as the distinctive markings on an animal's hide. Clothing can indicate to others where on the social ladder we belong. The colour of a shirt or top can be a signal of our personality. The amount of cleavage on display or the tightness of a skirt can be a projection of our self-image. The carrying of a designer handbag that has set someone back a month's salary can indicate such personal insecurity that only a branded bag will make them feel good – or it can simply mark the generosity of a rich boyfriend.

Jewellery is used to make statements about where on the journey of life we are: engagement rings, wedding rings, eternity rings all celebrate different points in a relationship. Inherited real jewellery can be worn as is, demonstrating loyalty to the family, or be remounted. Something as simple as the pen with which we write says a lot about us. A Mont Blanc fountain pen, for example, sends out a very different message, deliberately or accidentally, to the message sent by a chewed Bic.

Many companies now have rules about what their staff may or may not wear, even if they don't demand that staff wear a uniform. Wearing tights and make-up is considered basic grooming in some firms, whereas failure to observe dressdown Friday, with its requirement to arrive in jeans and a polo shirt, can mark you out as an over-formal nerd in other organisations.

It was ever thus. What people wore always gave others instantly-understood information about the wearer's role and social status.

In the Middle Ages jugglers, executioners and prostitutes were the ones who wore broad stripes. It marked them as individuals outside the respectable circles within society. They had their function, and their stripes not only marked them out for anyone who wished to avail of that function, but just as importantly, marked those who did not wear broad stripes as more respectable: a good bourgeois merchant tended to wear plain colours.

In fact, the dodginess of stripes went further. If you think of a cartoon about convicts, or even remember seeing the movie *O Brother, Where Art Thou?* you'll immediately draw to the eye of the mind a striped convict outfit, which, like the other uses of stripes, helped identify an escaped convict to the law-abiding citizen while delivering personal ignominy to the wearer, who was reduced to a highly visible generic state by the prison uniform. Nowhere was that prison uniform more effective in reducing prisoners to a category than in photographs of inmates in Nazi concentration camps, where the officers, in their spit-and-polish boots and pressed uniforms, look like a different species to the skeletal bestriped prisoners.

Historian Laurence Rees has recorded that one of the prisoners who survived Auschwitcz remembered having to cope, in addition to all his other tribulations, with a kind of reverse racism: 'For when he first saw German soldiers dressed in steel helmets and smart uniforms he felt they were "better" people; "And at the other side of the spectrum I've seen Jews or Poles afraid, running and hiding."'

This attitude, of course, is precisely the one the Germans hoped to create among those they wanted to oppress. It is one of the reasons Dr Mengele appeared on the ramp at Auschwitz immaculately dressed in his SS uniform, his boots shining like mirrors. For, just as the Germans wanted to create a self-fulfilling prophecy that those whom they fought were inferior, so by dressing and acting as if they were members of a master race they wanted to force their enemies to subscribe to the belief that the Nazis were indeed their superiors.

Military uniforms have had an enormous influence on fashion, particularly in businesses where authority was needed. In the early days of aviation, it was no accident that pilots wore uniforms (and still wear uniforms) evocative of the dress worn by officers in armies. Passengers felt more comfortable when the person flying the plane looked as if they were in command and accustomed to being in command. Men dressing for business, please take note. When someone advises you to wear an unstructured jacket made of linen, run a mile. You will look as if you've been sleeping under a bridge for the previous month.

Professional advice on what to wear is more widely available than at any time in the past. Historically, the advice you got came in the form of tradition or poverty. Tradition dictated that, for example, if you were royalty, you were allowed to wear fabrics and colours that the lower orders were not allowed to wear, even if they could afford silk or mink, which they couldn't.

Today, the web is full of make-over specialists, who have taken generations of women's magazine wisdom like 'wear white next to the face,' and 'darker colours make you look thinner' into a satisfying if expensive drama which sees them lay waste to your existing wardrobe before laying waste to your existing bank account to replace what they have excised.

The best advice I ever got about clothes, down through the years, amounts to these snippets:

- Save yourself ironing, if you use a drier, by tossing in five really damp small items like underpants or hankies just before you take out items like t-shirts. They'll help de-wrinkle the bulk of the items.

- Buy yourself a fabric-relaxer like Wrinkles Away, so that when you're travelling, you don't have to rig up a travel iron in order to present a sharp appearance.
- A tailored shirt always works. (That one's courtesy of the late Joe Lynch.)
- If you haven't worn something for a year, toss it.
- When you lose weight, lose your 'fat' clothes. Their very presence provides an incentive to get fat all over again.
- Use double-sided tape to prevent gaps between buttons on a shirt or button-through dress.
- Never buy a wraparound dress. They make thin women look skeletal and well-endowed women look fat.
- Never wear four-inch heels when going to a venue with cobblestones.
- Get a mirror that shows you your back view and take it seriously.
- Remember, when you fit into something at dawn, to take account of the lattes and edibles you may consume throughout the day which could result in your strangling on your waistband by nightfall.

Ann Rule, crime author
Attractive defendants traditionally have much less chance of being sentenced to death than those who look dangerous.

William Hazlitt, eighteenth-century essayist
Those who make their dress a principal part of themselves, will, in general, become of no more value than their dress.

Angela Carter, author
…it takes a helluva lot of guts to maintain oneself in a perpetual state of visual offensiveness.

Dolly Parton, country singer
It takes a lot of money to look this cheap.

Suetonius, Roman historian
Caesar pushed his scanty locks forward to conceal his bald scalp, and, of all the honors voted him by the senate and people there was none which he received or made use of more gladly than the privilege of wearing a laurel wreath at all times.

Pope John XXIII
(apologising for how long a photographic session had delayed him)
I don't understand the Lord. I don't understand God at all. He knew from all eternity that I would be Pope. Why, then, didn't he make me more photogenic?

George Burns, comedian
Be sure to wear a good cologne, a nice aftershave lotion and a strong underarm deodorant. And it might be a good idea to wear some clothes, too.

Dress simply. If you wear a dinner jacket, don't wear anything else on it. Like lunch or dinner.

15

ADVICE FROM THE PROFESSIONALS

From the earliest times, almost everywhere in the world, professional advice-givers made money out of answering the questions of the lovelorn, personally-distressed or career-oriented.

The Oracle at Delphi was one such professional. According to myth, a shepherd named Coretas observed that his sheep and goats started to go nuts whenever they approached a particular area to graze. When he followed them, he, too, began to act strangely, making prophetic statements which, as time progressed, turned out to be accurate.

In fact, the Priestesses of Daphoene, perhaps four centuries before Apollo, had operated in the vicinity of the area where he'd brought his sheep and goats to forage. Cross the palm of the Priestess with silver or gold, ask her a question and you'd certainly get an answer. You wouldn't be able to understand the answer, because the Priestess was spectacularly incoherent, so an assistant stood by to interpret what she had said and how it related to your life. Some of these instantaneous translaters sensibly made their own lives easier by asking questioners to put their query in a form that could be satisfied with a Yes or No answer. (Bit like the disembodied voice of directory enquiries who asks if you want the number texted to your mobile phone.)

When the Christians came along, they knew competition when they saw it. First of all, the faith they were spreading had to contend with the personally-directed statements of the Priestesses of the Serpent Oracles of Mother Goddess who presided at Delphi. Secondly, those asking the binary questions were pouring money into the Oracle. The Christians promptly rubbished the Priestess. Her incoherence, they said, was because she was drunk as a skunk on volcanic fumes escaping from the underground cavern. The priest who interpreted her words picked whatever translation would most please the supplicant in front of the Oracle. This latter claim seems to have been supported by Socrates, who made a lengthy speech about the fact that if you asked the Oracle who was the wisest man in the world, the oracle would tell you straight that it was yourself.

Much the same system as the one operated by the Queen in *Snow White and the Seven Dwarfs*, who had daily conversations with her own mirror. 'Mirror, mirror on the wall,' she would begin, once the make-up was on and the hair gelled, 'Who is the fairest of them all?'

The mirror, which knew which nail it was hanging on, would tell the Queen that she was the fairest by a country mile. Until Snow White became competition in the looks department and the mirror started to tell the truth.

Socrates not only didn't believe he was the wisest person in Greece at the time; he didn't believe the Oracle was all she was cracked up to be, either. That did not stop thousands of people visiting the site and seeking her advice. Nor did it stop the hundreds of thousands of tourists who, every year, visit the spectacular beauty spot in memory of her role as a gibberish advice-giver.

During the Dark Ages, advice – whether on herbs to ingest in order to get pregnant or on methods of seducing a potential mate

– was sought from the local 'wise woman'. These women knew everything from hallucinogenic preparations to the best method of ensuring safe childbirth. The Christian Church, once it had taken on the role of advice-giver and law-maker, did not like these old women at all. Nor did the emerging (male) profession of medicine. Never was a market so brutally won as during the witch craze which swept Europe (including, to some extent, Ireland) killing off any woman suspected of casting spells or of possessing abstruse pagan knowledge. It wasn't ethnic cleansing. It was gender cleansing, unprecedented and horrific, leaving whole villages in Europe barren of women and – at the same time – wiping out generations of race memory related to the medicinal use of plants.

It wasn't until the middle of the nineteenth century that women again began to make a lot of money out of advice-giving. Isabella Beeton, who died before she was thirty, was the doyenne of that century's dispensers of wisdom, although how much of it was her own and how much was cut-and-paste has never been clear. Isabella had started her publishing career by earning pin money crafting features for her publisher husband's magazines. Her tome on *Household Management* sold an unprecedented 60,000 copies in its first year and went on to become an essential in properly-run homes.

Sir Arthur Conan Doyle, the creator of Sherlock Holmes (himself no mean advice-giver to the unfortunate and permanently patronised Watson), said that Isabella's book 'has more wisdom to the square inch than any work of man'. Although the book is stuffed with recipes, it also touches on relationships:

> In conversation, one should never dwell unduly on
> the petty annoyances and disappointments of the day.
> Many people, almost unconsciously, get into the habit

of talking incessantly of the worries of servants and children, not realising that to many of their hearers these are worrisome subjects. It is unwise to start a topic concerning which you lack sufficient knowledge to discuss it with intelligence. Important events, whether of joy or sorrow, should be told to friends whose sympathy or congratulation may be welcome. The discreet wife will never allow a word about any fault of her husband to pass her lips – even the best husbands in this imperfect world, alas, have faults!

Mrs Beeton believed that friendships should not be hastily formed. (She'd have had serious reservations about speed-dating.) While it was, she held, important to meet people as a way of preventing oneself from becoming narrow-minded, it was equally important to be selective, always giving a thumbs-down to gossips: 'Acquaintances who indulge in scandal about neighbours and common friends should be avoided as a pestilence.'

Newspaper publishers in the United States got the Mrs Beeton message. Recipes were good. Hints on how to clean household items were good. But best of all was advice on manners and matters of the heart. Letters to the lovelorn had been a staple of eighteenth-century magazines. As the newspaper business took off in the early twentieth century, all editors began to include would now be called agony-aunt columns. Chicago, in particular, spawned one fascinating double act. Two sisters, Esther and Pauline Friedman, starting in journalism in Chicago, became better known as Ann Landers and 'Dear Abby', dominating the agony-aunt franchise and, in a sense, defining it.

Identical twins, born in Sioux City, Iowa, in 1918, they both studied journalism and got together to provide a gossip column for a local newspaper, before dropping out of university to stage a double wedding, after which their relationship cooled, not least because they were career competitors.

'Eppie' Lederer took over the advice column which had been written by a nurse who had died, keeping the name under which the nurse had operated, Ann Landers. From the moment she took it over, in 1955, it was a major and eventually a national success.

Pauline, started out helping her sister and then decided to go her own way. In 1956, under the pen name Abigail Van Buren, she started to contribute an agony-aunt column to the *San Francisco Chronicle*. The two newspapers for which they wrote competed ferociously with each other, as did the two sisters. Their good counsel started with off-the-top-of-their-heads tips and wrinkles, but, over time, developed so that each had a bank of professionals, including doctors, psychiatrists and psychologists, on whose expertise they could draw. Landers had an edge to her writing and was enormously popular, receiving, on average, 2,000 letters per day.

Although they wrote under false names, neither made a secret of their profession. Some agony columnists, however, choose to remain anonymous. Sometimes this happens because the newspaper involved doesn't want to be overly committed to one named person – it's easier to have a brand name on the column, which can be written by a series of anonymous scribes. Some newspapers believe that readers get distracted, not just by the appearance and personality of an advice-giver who appears in other media, but because they like to believe that the advice-giver has a perfect life. The agony-aunt's credibility, for many readers, lies in the assumption that they've never made a mistake.

That didn't stop Ann Landers from coming clean about her own failed marriage. When her husband left her for another woman, it was, she always maintained, the greatest trauma of her life. Shortly after the separation started, she wrote an unusually short column. At the bottom of the text she submitted to her editor, she added a personal note, asking that the white space occasioned by the shorter column be left blank, with a message to readers saying that the printed silence was her way of honouring 'one of the world's best marriages that didn't make it to the finish line'.

The best bit of advice I got, when I edited my first magazine – *Nikki*, a teenage glossy put out by the Creation Group – was: 'Take the agony-aunt column seriously.'

I told the older journalist giving the advice that I had no intention of having an agony-aunt column. She smiled at me. 'You can't not have an advice column, no matter what you call it,' she told me. 'Just as you can't not have a horoscope.'

In due course, I got the same message, rather more forcefully, from my bosses on the magazine. Fortunately, I happened on a freelance journalist who wrote both horoscope and advice column and took the stars and the personal agonies equally seriously. Once I'd seen some of the letters going to her, I understood the older journalist's wisdom. A jokey or ironic approach to advice would have wounded lonely and frightened people already disadvantaged in some way.

The advice column in any magazine is self-selecting. Cynics assume that the more spectacular, florid problems are made up by the editorial staff, but in my experience, this isn't the case. The letters that stop you in your tracks are patently genuine. But the kind of letters a magazine catering to middle-class middle-aged women will get are obviously different in tone and content to the letters received by magazines aimed at a younger, more 'laddish' audience.

Angela McNamara was the agony aunt most of the older people in Ireland remember, from the days when she had almost a full page to herself in the then *Sunday Press*. Mrs McNamara was, and still is, strongly Catholic. Logically, her first ventures into publication appeared in a Catholic magazine called *The Irish Messenger*. At the time, she was also speaking in secondary schools about questions of morals.

This was in the sixties, when the Pill had freed women to be sexually active, when television had reduced the insularity of Ireland, and when the narrow morality recorded in the novel *The Valley of the Squinting Windows* was giving way to a new set of behaviours, particularly among teenagers.

It was in this context that Angela Mc Namara started an advice column that was to run for almost two decades, and make her name synonymous with proper Catholic sexual mores. When the *Sunday Press* died, Angela McNamara went from household name to nostalgic reference.

She continued to visit schools, make occasional media appearances and to write, publishing an autobiographical book in recent years. In that book, she offers samples of the kind of questions she got in the sixties, comparing them with typical questions twenty and more years later. All had changed, changed utterly: whereas in the sixties, one teenager was agonised about the fact that her mother wanted a favourite poster of Adam Faith removed from her bedroom wall, by the nineties, a twelve-year-old was asking "What age can you start using condoms?"

Indeed, the last century may have been the final period in human history where parental and grandparental advice was the main source of information about acceptable behaviour. The telephone was the first nail in that coffin: kids could communicate directly with each other at all times of the day and night, and so peer-to-peer advice became at least as important as parental advice. Then came the Internet, with its limitless supply of advice, good, bad and indifferent, on every topic from sex to starving. Particularly starving.

Innumerable websites now offer teenagers tips and wrinkles on how to get through a day on two or three hundred calories, supported by pictures – usually of girls – emaciated to skeletons.

16

Advice on Dying

Here's an oddity.

Dying is the one activity we all have to undertake. It's also the one about which not one single person of those I contacted for this book had any advice, either to offer anybody else, or that they'd received from another individual. It could be suggested that this dearth of good advice derives from the fact that, once someone has done the dying thing, they're not in a great position to come back and tell the rest of us the best way to go about it.

But it may also stem from our individual and several belief that dying affects everyone except ourselves. Until we get a diagnosis which specifically limits the time we have on this earth, we avoid thinking about death. Or we refer to it in jokey terms like:

- Pop our clogs
- Put on the wooden overcoat
- Sleep with the fishes
- Get wasted
- Bite the dust

It comes as no consolation, in the context of that denial, to learn that more ways of dying are available to us, if you go by death certificates, than were vouchsafed our forefathers. Three centuries ago, people were certified as dying from one of three hundred causes. Today, we die from up to three thousand ailments, accidents or self-administered methods.

We also tend to die in hospitals or hospices, whereas up to about a hundred years ago, people died at home, surrounded by their families.

Dr Elizabeth Kübler-Ross is the source of much of the advice terminally ill people get about dying. Kübler-Ross, who was Swiss, studied medicine even though her parents didn't want her to, and ended up working as a psychiatrist in the United States. Her book, *On Death and Dying*, published in 1969, heavily influenced how the terminally-ill are cared for, but, as she explained in an interview recorded before her death in 2004, her fascination with how people cope with personal mortality began a lot earlier:

> It started in Maidanek, in a concentration camp, where I tried to see how children had gone into the gas chambers after having lost their families, their homes, their schools and everything. The walls in the camp were filled with pictures of butterflies, drawn by these children. It was incomprehensible to me. Thousands of children going into the gas chamber, and this is the message they leave behind – a butterfly. That was really the beginning.

Kübler-Ross, many years after her visit to the concentration camp, found herself working with terminally-ill patients in Chicago, where she began to make notes about what they required and what they often didn't get from the friends, family and professionals surrounding them. One of the key strictures she developed concerned how much the dying should be told about their state:

You have to be honest, but you don't have to be totally honest. You have to answer their questions, but don't volunteer information for which they have not asked, because that means they're not ready for it yet. If somebody thinks you're a good guy if you tell them the whole truth, that there's nothing else we can do, this is baloney. Without miracles, there are many, many ways of helping somebody, without a cure. So you have to be very careful how you word it. And you never, ever, ever take hope away from a dying patient. Without hope nobody can live. You are not God. You don't know what else is in store for them, what else can help them, or how meaningful, maybe, the last six months of a person's life are. Totally changed around. So you don't just go and drown them in 'truth'. My golden rule has been to answer all the questions as honestly as I can. If they ask me statistically what are their chances...I had a wonderful teacher, who once said that of his patients 50 percent live one year, another 35 percent live two years, and another so-and-so many per cent live two and a half years, and so on. If you were very smart and added all the percentages up, there was always one per cent left. And the real shrewd ones said, 'Hey, you forgot, what about that last one per cent?' And he always said, 'The last per cent is for hope.' I like that. He never gave it to them with 100 per cent. He was fantastic.

It only depends how you have lived. If you have lived fully, then you have no regrets, because you have done the best you can do. If you made lots of goofs

– much better to have made lots of goofs than not to have lived at all. The saddest people I see die are people who had parents who said, 'Oh, I would be so proud if I can say "my son the doctor." ' They think they can buy love by doing what mom tells them to do and what dad tells them to do. They never listen to their own dreams. And they look back and say, 'I made a good living but I never lived.' That, to me, is the saddest way to live.

That's why I tell people, and I really mean it literally, if you're not doing something that really turns you on, do something that does turn you on, and you will be provided for to survive. Those people die with a sense of achievement, of priding themselves that they had the guts to do it.

Kübler-Ross observed that most people, when they knew they were dying, went through a series of emotional stages in their struggle to cope. Directly after learning of the diagnosis, for example, they tended to go into denial: this can't be happening to me, they have it wrong.

The next step was anger: I never smoked or allowed myself to get out of shape. This is so unfair. This, for many patients, led to envy of people who were still – as the dying person saw it – undeservedly enjoying good health and the prospect of a long life.

Thereafter came bargaining. This one, she admitted, was the most difficult to study, because, especially in religious patients, it took the form of frantic prayer, of asking God for survival or – in some cases – for at least postponement of the death until some significant event had been reached.

Realism would then set in, often accompanied by depression.

(People suffering depression are often grimly realistic.) Patients would go through a period of mourning for what they were about to lose, weeping that they would never see their children marry and have children of their own, or grieving for achievements that they would now never accomplish.

Finally, the patient would reach the stage of acceptance, coming to terms with the inevitability of their own demise and taking charge of it to whatever degree was possible. Acceptance often led to a great sense of peace, and sometimes even of joy, in the dying person.

These phases varied with the individual. Some experienced them in a single day-long rush, some went through them, looping back and forth, for several months. Why they mattered, experts in care of the dying maintain, is that knowledge of these phases in the dying process can improve the sensitivity with which doctors, nurses and family approach the patient.

It doesn't always have that payoff. My dearest friend and colleague, Collette Cullen, after she had been told that the cancer from which she suffered would kill her within a year, was visited by a specialist nurse. 'I'm not going to die within a year,' Collette told the nurse, before outlining a series of things she had planned, which would take at least eighteen months. The nurse shook her head and told her that she was in the denial phase of the stages of dying. Collette, with great charm and matching firmness, indicated that a) she wasn't and b) she was sure this formulaic approach (not that she called it that) would be very helpful to many patients, but she didn't find it that helpful. She then went on to live even longer than she had promised and to do even more than she had aimed to.

Bottom line? If Kübler-Ross's stages of dying can be helpful to you or to someone you're caring for when they're dying, use them. If not, don't.

For too many people suffering from diseases like cancer, the period before they start to die is more painful than the dying itself. That's because of 'opiophobia,' a fear on the part of medics that overuse of narcotics will cause addiction. If you are dying, or taking care of someone who is dying, one good piece of advice, issued quietly by many GPs, is: don't stay with a doctor who has opiophobia. Insist on being pain-free.

One of the most interesting books about dying was written by a doctor named George Sheehan, who had become world famous for his passion for running and his belief that it could radically improve the health and happiness of many of his patients. When Sheehan was diagnosed with terminal cancer, he found himself, as he put it, 'heckled' by physical symptoms from when he woke until he went to bed. He was miserable and frightened, until he took a phone call from a physician friend who lived on the other side of the United States. The friend asked him how he was doing, and Sheehan told him bluntly that the symptoms he was suffering were ruining what life was left to him. His friend's advice was succinct: take enough morphine to relieve the pain; take enough cortisone to slow your reaction to the tumor. 'That will get you six months,' he said, 'then we'll talk about it again.'

Sheehan was astonished to find how well this worked, even though he knew, from various signs and from the tests taken in the hospital, that his tumours were growing and his life shortening. But the cortisone dampened down the worse of the symptoms, and the morphine helped with the pain. Or, as Sheehan wrote, just a few months before he died, 'I take one [morphine] dose in the morning and one at night. Pain is now no more than a rumour…'

That's how it should be, for all patients who know they are to die from cancer or similar diseases. This determination to control pain so that it is no more than a rumour, allowing the patient to spend meaningful time with friends and family, and to reflect on their own life, is what has made the hospice movement so powerful in its approach to the dying process.

For some people, of course, the best advice about dying is how not to. In plane crashes, for instance, where several passengers survive a crash and conflagration, while many others with an equal chance of escape end up dead, often sitting in their seats. The survival instinct seems to be stronger in some people than in others. In any disaster, the sense that someone else is in charge – or should be in charge – seems to disempower people from taking control of their own escape, whereas other passengers on the same plane climb over the backs of seats or scoot along the floor where the lights can help them to an exit, with or without instruction from cabin staff. Resignation to impending death seems to contribute to its arrival.

That was one of the reasons Ernest Shackleton, the man whose Antarctic journey gave rise to the aptly titled book, *The Worst Journey in the World*, worked so hard to keep morale high and discipline rigorous, making sure the scientists within the marooned party focused on the experiments and tests they were supposed to undertake, even if they secretly believed nobody would ever benefit from or know about their findings. Shackleton ensured that the crew got out of bed at the same time each morning. He may or may not have known that staying in bed, failing to wash, refusing to engage with the quotidian, are all to often signs of surrender to mortality among the stressed, whether in a concentration camp, in the aftermath of a shipwreck or when part of a lost expedition in freezing conditions.

Alexander Donat, a Holocaust survivor, credited the survival of himself and some friends to the fact that they saved a little of the phoney coffee they received each morning and used it to wash themselves. The prisoners who drank all the coffee died sooner. 'This was the first step to the grave,' Donat wrote. 'It was almost an iron law: those who failed to wash every day soon died.'

Advice about dying is fairly plentiful. Advice from the dead is also in good supply. Some of it comes in the form of a will – those making wills have frequently used their bequests to send approving or disapproving guidance to their survivors. The desire to control the lives of others after one has ceased to be is a weird and apparently ineradicable factor in humanity. It's balanced by the desire to comfort the bereaved after one's own death.

The classic example of the latter is a letter like this, from a Private Jesse Givens, who died in Iraq in 2007, leaving this letter for his wife Melissa, his six-year-old stepson Dakota, and his son Carson (nicknamed Bean) who was born three weeks after his father died.

My family
I never thought that I would be writing a letter like this. I really don't know where to start. I've been getting bad feelings, though, and, well, if you are reading this…

The happiest moments in my life all deal with my little family. I will always have with me the small moments we all shared. The moments when you quit taking life so serious and smiled. The sounds of a beautiful boy's laughter or the simple nudge of a baby unborn. You will never know how complete you have made me. You saved me from loneliness and taught me how to think beyond myself. You taught me how to live and to love. You opened my eyes to a world I never dreamed existed.

Dakota…you taught me how to care until it

hurts, you taught me how to smile again. You taught me that life isn't so serious and sometimes you just have to play. You have a big, beautiful heart. Through life you need to keep it open and follow it. Never be afraid to be yourself. I will always be there in our park when you dream so we can play. I love you, and hope someday you will understand why I didn't come home. Please be proud of me.

Bean, I never got to see you but I know in my heart you are beautiful. I know you will be strong and big-hearted like your mom and brother. I will always have with me the feel of the soft nudges on your mom's belly, and the joy I felt when I found out you were on your way. I love you, Bean.

Melissa, I have never been as blessed as the day I met you. You are my angel, soulmate, wife, lover and best friend. I am sorry. I did not want to have to write this letter. There is so much more I need to say, so much more I need to share. A lifetime's worth. I married you for a million lifetimes. That's how long I will be with you. Please keep my babies safe. Please find it in your heart to forgive me for leaving you alone…Teach our babies to live life to the fullest, tell yourself to do the same.

I will always be there with you, Melissa. I will always want you, need you and love you, in my heart, my mind and my soul. Do me a favor, after you tuck the children in. Give them hugs and kisses from me. Go outside and look at the stars and count them. Don't forget to smile.

Love always

Your husband, Jess

Woody Allen, film director
Dying is one of the few things that can be done as easily lying down.

George Sheehan, MD
People who know they have cancer have a motto: 'Make every day count.'
I have done that. What I have not done is make every person count. My
life has been filled with the best of me. What it has not been filled with is
the best of others.

Joan Didion, author
After my mother died I received a letter from a friend in Chicago, a former
Maryknoll priest, who precisely intuited what I felt. The death of a parent,
he wrote, 'despite our preparation, indeed, despite our age, dislodges
things deep in us, sets off reactions that surprise us and that may cut free
memories and feelings that we had thought gone to ground long ago...'

C.S. Lewis, author, after the death of his wife
I think I am beginning to understand why grief feels like suspense. It
comes from the frustration of so many impulses that had become habitual.
Thought after thought, feeling after feeling, action after action, had H. for
their object. Now their target is gone. I keep on through habit fitting an
arrow to the string, then I remember and have to lay the bow down. So
many roads lead thought to H. I set out on one of them. But now there's
an impassable frontierpost across it. So many roads once; now so many
cul de sacs.

Martha Gelhorn, author (who committed suicide in her eighties)
I have no grasp of time and no control over my memory. I cannot order it
to deliver. Unexpectedly, it flings up pictures, disconnected with no before
or after. It makes me feel a fool. What is the use in having lived so long,
traveled so widely, listened and looked so hard, if in the end you don't
know what you know?

Dr Leale (who was present when Lincoln was dying)
Knowledge that frequently just before departure recognition and reason return to those who have been unconscious, caused me for several hours to hold the president's right hand firmly within my grasp, to let him in his blindness know, if possible, that he was in touch with humanity and had a friend.

Bryan Murray, actor
Maybe it's the actor in me but the first time I heard the saying, 'Life's not a rehearsal – this is it,' it stopped me in my tracks. It was the early eighties, I was a young actor just moved to London and I had been recommended a 'Life' seminar called the 'est training' by some friends. After a lot of fearful prognostication I finally did it. It turned out to be one of the richest experiences of my life.

The saying sums up, for me at any rate, the spirit of the seminar and what its creator, a man called Werner Erhardt, wanted to share and express through it. Sitting there in the seminar I realised that I was waiting for certain things to happen in order for my life to start. A good career, few bob in the bank, a nice place to live etc, etc. But if this was it then there was no point in waiting around. Life had started. It's on!

It seemed to me to be an invitation to participate more fully in life. It was a scary but exciting thought. And I bored everyone to death with it for about five years after. The seminar was not intended nor did it make me happier, thinner or better in bed. It did give me a greater sense of aliveness though than I had before for which I am eternally grateful. Even now twenty-five years later life is still scary but exciting.

I'll miss it when it's over.